Paul Adrian M

DELIVER US

FROM EVIL

SING TO THE LORD AND DANCE WITH THE DEVIL

Printed in the United States of America

ISBN: Softcover   979-8-88622-053-7
             eBook   979-8-88622-054-4

Republished by: PageTurner Press and Media LLC

Publication Date: 03/02/2022

To order copies of this book, contact:

PageTurner Press and Media

Phone: 1-888-447-9651

info@pageturner.us

www.pageturner.us

The cover photograph

In 2004, I stayed at the Hilton Hotel, opposite Central Station, Belfast. As I gazed out upon the landscape of East Belfast, I noticed the two Giant Cranes (Samson & Goliath) of Harland & Wolff Shipyard in the distance. I immediately thought of the tragedy of the Titanic from that shipyard. I also remembered the years of terror that the troubles had brought to Northern Ireland, and I prayed,

"Where are you, Lord, in all of this?

Immediately a colossal Rainbow appeared in the sky over East Belfast and the two cranes, and I heard the Lord say,

"I bring hope to the people of Belfast."

I took photographs of the 'Rainbow of Hope' on that day and filed them away. Now I know why.

DEDICATION

This book is dedicated firstly to the glory of God, who continually delivers me from evil, and to the memory of my mother, who taught me that He would always do so.

Also, to a little 9-year-old lad, Sean Flood, whose enthusiasm and ability to see things in a different light will consistently remind me to stay positive in all situations.

PREFACE

The book you are about to read is a true story, not written to scare anyone, but written as a warning to both the Seeker and the Believer. What I have written is also not meant to attribute blame. The Blame Game started in the Garden of Eden and continues today. However, it is written firstly as a warning about the cost of one's decisions in this life, and more so, to prove that God can and will deliver us from all evil if we trust in Him to do so because we will always be His children – no matter what we do.

As you delve into the content within these pages, I pray it will inspire you to have faith in the God of the multiple chances, who is neither Catholic nor Protestant nor, for that matter, any religious organization but is a spirit who can reign within us. In Luke 17:21 (KJV), Jesus said, "The Kingdom of God is within you."

We are created to worship Him in Spirit and Truth. In saying that, I would remind the reader that the term 'Hereafter' consists of two words. What you do in the former will reflect in the latter

Some names and places in this book are changed to keep both innocent and guilty anonymous and protect me from possible litigation or death. I would request that anyone who knows or thinks that they know to whom I am referring would also respect my wishes for anonymity. You will laugh, and you will cry. You will be happy, and you will be angry.

You will be surprised and sometimes even shocked but understand that the facts are absolutely the truth, the whole truth, and nothing but the truth.

Having reached the age of seventy-four, one of the many things I have learned along the 'sometimes bitter' road of life through this crazy world is that one never will know what is around the next bend. It may be an incredibly unique and glorious vista or, possibly, a picture of destruction and carnage. What we need desperately on that road and in those times is a friend, a true friend who will never let us down, never point the finger, accept us as who we are, and love us despite all our faults. A friend who will pick us up every single time we trip and fall as we surely will. In the telling of this story, you will find out about mine.

INTRODUCTION

An ancient adage declares that the same water which softens the potato hardens the egg.

What makes you who you are, not your circumstances, will determine your outcome.

Now, that may be a great piece of distilled wisdom, but not much help when you are **in** the boiling water.

During the Summer of 2010, I had the immense pleasure of meeting the famous Bill Cullen at the 15th Anniversary Celebrations of the Professional Insurance Brokers Association (PIBA) in the Radisson Hotel, Stillorgan, Dublin, where he was the Keynote Speaker

The conversation progressed to my upbringing in Belfast and what it was like during "The Troubles" in Northern Ireland. On discovering that I had been born on the Falls Road in Belfast, he told me that he was taking a group of underprivileged children from the Lower Falls in Belfast on a trip the following week.

He then produced an old tattered black and white photograph of a large group of children and asked me to spot the one with the shoes on. There wasn't one. "That's my family and pals with whom I grew up, in Summerhill, Dublin," he smiled, "I keep that photograph close to my heart to remind me of my roots. We need humility in this world."

At that particular time, Bill was CEO of the largest Motor Group in Ireland, Glencullen Holdings, with a turnover of €350 million at its peak. He owned a very prosperous 5-star hotel, Killegy House, Muckross Park, Killarney, and was purchasing another one.

As if that didn't keep him busy, he was also the Principal and founder of the first Entrepreneurial College in Ireland, the Europa Academy located at Balheary Road, Swords near Dublin Airport. He had also become a renowned author, with one of his books, "It's a long way from Penny Apples," making it to the top on both sides of the Atlantic. Along with Jackie Lavin, his spouse, he hosted the Apprentice on RTE Television.

Bill lost everything when the property boom and the banks collapsed during the economic downturn. Thankfully, he has pulled himself up by the boot laces and has a thriving business again.

But meeting this fantastic person taught me that life is unpredictable and what is in your heart and your belief pattern will take you where you need to go in this life.

Life is not about how many times you fall; it's about how many times you rise again.

In 1937 Napoleon Hill published his now-famous book, "Think and Grow Rich," wherein may be found his famous quotation, "Whatever the mind can conceive and believe it can achieve." I would rearrange that prose somewhat to "Whatever grows in your heart, and you fervently believe in, you will achieve it, whether good or evil."

My mother used to tell me, "Don't tell lies, Paul, you don't have a good enough memory. However, you will always remember the truth. As you grow older, you will realize that there are three sides to every story, his and her's, and then the truth. Seek after truth - always."

*****

On my various travels throughout my life, I have met many persons of varying faiths and cultures, most of them, thankfully, beautiful and sincere human beings, full of love, empathy, and kindness.

I understand (*most of the time*) why these loving people have the faith that they follow. That understanding mostly comes down to one of two reasons, their parents raised them that way, or they had a life-changing 'Eureka' moment when they changed their opinion and took a different path in life.

I have met or know some, even amongst family and friends, who purport to be either 'Atheist or Agnostic' and have no time whatsoever for "Bible Thumpers" and "Those who wish to proselytize them." and, again, I understand, (*most of the time*).

An atheist disbelieves in a Divine Being, and an agnostic neither believes nor disbelieves in any god. Agnostics assert that humans can't know anything about the universe's creation or if divine beings exist.

The most challenging and stubborn people I find difficult to converse with on this subject are the 'Religious,' who have their preconceived ideas and way of life and are not prepared to examine someone else's opinion or point of view. The minds of these people are closed tight, and a closed umbrella becomes useless unless one opens it during the rain.

The types of characters whom Jesus had all the trouble with would have been the religious leaders, the Pharisees, Sadducees, and the Scribes, who followed strict codes to the letter according to their interpretation. What do I mean by that? It all depends on how they looked at the Law and how God made it. The glass of water can be half full and half empty – both views are correct - but which picture do you take? Call your wife a kitten, and she will purr but call her a cat, and she'll scratch your eyes out.

However, that is not my concern. The ones whom I am addressing in this book are those who are lost, the lonely, the broken, the depressed, the people especially who have been hurt by the 'Religious,' and who are seeking for the truth, the answers to the questions that they have been asking to an uncaring skyline for a long time.

You, Dear One, could be one of these desperate souls seeking the answers to the age-old questions, "Is there a God, and if there is, why doesn't He help me? Does He even care about me? Why is the world so evil? What will happen when I die?" Many questions may remain unanswered from your times of trouble. Do you happen to be one of this group? Are you fed up with all the confusion, conflict, and caustic bigotry of this world? If so, I believe that this book will be of immense help and comfort to your aching heart. I pray that you will obtain the answers to your questions and allow some modicum of peace to return to your life and to renew your hope and faith in the God of multiple chances, who loves you beyond measure.

No matter what we believe or don't believe, at one time or another, I am pretty sure that everyone has stumbled over the question, "What am I doing here?" When we find God, we learn the answers to these difficult questions. But it is a slow process, usually built over a lifetime of changing experiences on our journey. Just remember two things, an open mind will discover more than a closed mind, and God turns up in the strangest of places, not always in Church.

I met Cardinal Daly once in his home in Armagh. I was making a delivery to his housekeeper, and he came into the kitchen. I found him to be a man who was at peace with himself and the world after a short discussion about how God can turn up when one is really in trouble. He told me a story of a vagrant sitting at the bottom of the long steps of Armagh Cathedral, and he was crying bitterly. Suddenly Jesus came walking along the footpath,

"What's wrong, my dear Brother?" He said to the vagrant.

"They won't let me in there," cried the poor man.

"Oh, don't worry about that," smiled Jesus, "I haven't been in there in years."

"Mind you!" laughed Cardinal Daly to me, "That was before my time."

*****

Mention the name, "C.S. Lewis," and it conjures up stories from the seven classics in the Chronicles of Narnia, such as 'The Lion the Witch and the Wardrobe,' Prince Caspian,' 'The voyage of the Dawn Treader', plus another four books in the series.

The Narnia books alone have sold over a hundred million copies and produced three successful films.

Lewis was born in East Belfast, Northern Ireland, the son of Albert and Florence, who named him 'Clive Staples Lewis,' on the 29th November 1898. He attended Wynyard School, Watford, England, and continued his education at Campbell College, Belfast. At eighteen, he was awarded a scholarship to University College, Oxford, in 1916.

He eventually became a Fellow at Magdalen College, Oxford, and a tutor in English Literature until 1954. From 1954 to1963, he was a professor of Medieval and Renaissance English at Cambridge University.

Known lovingly as 'C.S,' Lewis was one of the most influential writers the 20th century ever produced. Before the massive success of the Narnia Volumes, written much later in Lewis's life, 1950 to 1956, he had written books under the 'Nom de Plumes' of 'Clive Hamilton and N.W. Clerk', obviously to protect his good name if they were a flop More than thirty-seven published works are attributed to him, three of them following his death in Jan 1963, aged 64.

What is the reason for relating all of this?

Well, it continues to amaze me the number of 'Educated & Intelligent' people whom I meet, who have made their mind up that there is no God, nor do they wish even to research the subject that He might just possibly exist. Most of them know many of their peer groups who have gone through a great deal of exploratory investigation on the subject. After the extensive and proven study, the various investigators have decided that there is a God, and not only that. He is also our 'Father in Heaven.'

Einstein declared that everybody is a genius, but if you judge a fish by its ability to climb a tree, it will lead its life believing that it is stupid. He also declared that condemnation without investigation is the epitome of stupidity. So, according to Einstein, these educated fools are stupid. The NIV Bible (*what I refer to as the 'Northern Ireland' Version*) even quotes in Psalm 14 verse 1, "The Fool says in his heart, 'There is no God'. They are corrupt, their deeds are vile, there is no one who does good".

I used to pass that poster on platform five at Connolly Station, Dublin, and wonder how many have noticed it. Not many, as it's not there anymore. Anyhow, maybe some of these dear souls (and perhaps *you are one of them ready to discard this book*) should take a look at the life of C.S Lewis and Einstein and read some of their quotes of wisdom or, even better, read a book or two. C.S wrote 'Mere Christianity after he converted to Christianity in September 1931. I am not sure if he ever met Einstein, who died in 1955, but he adhered to his advice.

In his book, 'Mere Christianity,' Lewis examines the proclaimed identity and the history of Jesus, not only from the Christian authors but also the Jewish, Greek, and Roman historians. He decided that he believed that the Hebrew 'Yeshua,' i.e. 'Jesus,' was, in fact, the Son of God and had become a man, like us who visited our planet over two thousand years ago. Although accepted and followed by thousands during His short ministry of three years, He was put to death by the Religious Hierarchy, using their Roman Conquerors (*their Enemy*) as executioners. He also discovered that they did not capture Jesus. The Lord gave himself over to be killed, as the Lamb of God, to die for us.

C.S Lewis was one of the world's greatest literary geniuses. Until his early thirties, he was also a confirmed atheist. This newly informed man devoted his life to proclaiming his findings through his books to the world. He also knew full well that the mainstream churches had muddied the waters of a simple message and had instigated their rules, regulations, embellishments, and human error, just like the Pharisees had done and became a stumbling block for those seeking Truth.

In 'The Screwtape Letters' published in 1942, Lewis creates the main character, 'Screwtape,' a senior Demon, that sends letters of instruction to his nephew, a junior demon named 'Wormwood' advising him how to bring the 'Patient's' soul successfully to hell and damnation. He states that Wormwood does not have to go to the trouble of organizing some major sin, "Why to use Adultery when Golf will do?'.

Screwtape explains the 'Law of Undulation,' a natural and common occurrence in a human's life suitable for Satan's advantage. The Law of Undulation dictates that a man or woman's life does not move forward in a straight line, and it undulates like a mathematical sine wave or a roller coaster. The most appropriate place for an attack is at the bottom and the top. Wormwood is to watch for the sudden change in pattern and start his planned attack, "Catch him at his very lowest ebb, where he feels worthless, filled with fear or remorse, even depression. You might get him on suicide, or, even better, turn him against God and over to us. The other opportunity is at his highest peak when he is prideful of his successes. Tempt him there with some juicy stuff, or on the other hand, drag him back down suddenly to the pit of despair where the pain will be worst because of the loss. Humans don't know that their journey is all valleys and peaks and will blame anyone but themselves, even God".

This rollercoaster could apply to you or me on life's journey. In our search for peace and contentment, we all long to be free of these natural conditions of the business of just living through life. Unfortunately, many folks do not include God in their daily lives, and they may know about Him, but they do not know Him personally.

Jesus responded to Philip's question, "Show us the Father" in John chapter 14 by saying, "Don't you know me, Philip, even after I have been among you such a long time? Anyone who has seen me has seen the Father..." (John 14:9 NIV).

For those who have handed their lives over to Jesus, who is not only our Lord and King but also our brother (*the bible refers to Him as 'The first of many Brethren'*), that longing can be satisfied, not only in the world to come but in this world as well.

The Ups and Downs will continue, the hurts will continue, even the temptation to sin will continue. But now we have a Brother and Friend alongside us to help us cope with life, someone who will never leave us or forsake us. He will even carry us when we are too exhausted to walk anymore. How do I know this? You ask. Because He has done it for me many times, you will hear all about it in the following fantastic story.

Be assured that the Ups and Downs will continue. That is an integral part of life. However, an up follows every down, and every Low is followed by a High. To complete the journey with Joy, I discovered that Jim Reeves' famous song was of tremendous help to me on my trip. (*Why not google it?*)

"This world is not my home. I'm just passing through.

My treasures are laid up somewhere beyond the blue."

(Songwriter Mary Reeves Davis, (1962), "This world is not my home" sung by Jim Reeves).

Your list of troubles could be long or short. No matter, hand it over to the Lord Jesus and don't you dare take it back, leave it there.

David, the shepherd king, prayed at his lowest valley,

"The Lord is My shepherd. I shall not want. Though I pass through the valley of the shadow of death, I will fear no evil: for thou art with me; thy rod and staff comfort me." (Psalm 23: 1&4)

There have been many days when those words were the only comfort that I clung to, a life raft when I was alone in the storms of life. During those times, that beautiful chorus, "Because He lives," penned by Bill and Gloria Gaither, reminded me that God loved me and sent His son, Jesus, to rescue me:

"Because He lives, I can face tomorrow.

Because He lives, all fear is gone.

Because I know He holds the future,

And life is worth the living, just because He lives."

Often those who hurt you the most are those who are closest to you, causing resentment and bitterness to grow in the hidden recesses of your heart. I know because it has happened more often than I care to remember, and I have also caused this pain to others. But, if we can learn to forgive one another, that pain subsides and eventually disappears. I have proven this over many years, and now it comes naturally. It is better and much easier to let God sort it than for me to be bothered trying to do it. My mother, whom you'll meet in this story, told me, "Paul, sour grapes make bitter wine. Holding a grudge is holding a red-hot ember in your hand, waiting to throw it at someone. Meantime, who is it burning?"

At the last supper, Jesus said, "A new commandment I give you, That ye love one another; as I have loved you, that ye also love one another." (John 13:34 KJV)

I hope you enjoy the story.

The Wolf at the Door

At around midnight, his concentration was interrupted when he thought he had heard a knock at the door, then a louder knock, followed by repeated knocking.

Who's that at this hour? Why are they knocking? What's wrong with the bell? Who's in trouble?

The unanswered questions spun in his head as Paul rushed to the door, a feeling of dark foreboding slowly starting to rise in the pit of his stomach.

Peter and Shirley Grower stood shivering in the cold under the dim light of the porch. The rain was pouring down behind them, rattling like a Lambeg Drum off the roof of Paul's new Saab in the driveway.

"Come in," Paul hugged Shirley and flung the door wide, "What on earth is the problem this hour of the night. Why didn't you ring the bell? Why didn't you phone?" the questions poured out of him to the silent couple.

Suddenly he realized that Shirley couldn't speak. Peter was the first to break the silence, "Shirley has lost her voice, and we are singing in the Ulster Hall tomorrow. We came in desperation hoping that you were still up and could pray for her".

"Peter, you are supposed to call for the Elders of the church. I am only a Deacon, and I'll ring one of them now", Paul preached at him as usual without thinking.

"I was instructed to come here," replied Peter a little more forcefully.

"Well, no harm in praying," Paul led them through the large oak hall, passed the carved staircase, and went into his study at the rear of the house. It was a granny flat with a separate bathroom and kitchen, which the previous owner had added to the house.

He was pretty proud of his home and his dramatic climb up the corporate ladder faster than expected. Since coming to the town penniless a few years previously, doors had just miraculously opened for him, eventually leading to the purchase of a large secluded semi-detached house in the upmarket end of town. Some people would say,

"The lad had done well,"

but Paul realized where his *blessings* originated.

As he had done many times before, Peter commented on the beautiful home how blessed Paul and his family were, adding what a gift both he and his wife and family were to the church, teaching Sunday school, involved in many ministries. The Church members had recently voted Paul onto the oversight as a Deacon. He was also the caretaker and worked in the Tape ministry to visit the old folks. Their homegroup was expanding, and Peter asked where he found time to clean and maintain the church, drive one of the minibusses and still be proficient in his career as the general manager of one of the oldest Finance Houses in Northern Ireland.

"Well, yes, I am on my feet again. Life is about getting up after you fall", Paul unashamedly allowed himself to preen a little.

His role in the Finance House as General Manager gave him the same credibility as a bank manager.

He was a member of the exclusive Reform Club in Royal Avenue, Belfast, after being introduced for membership by the famous Quinton Hogg from Lombard & Ulster Banking. Who would have imagined it, a college drop-out, leaving College with only two 'O' levels, French and English Literature, the only two subjects he had shown any interest in, could rise to such heights in any community?

It never occurred to him that his EGO, an acronym for *Edge God Out*, had started to rule his head, and now he was treading on thin ice once again. Unfortunately for him, as often before, pride comes before every fall.

Paul was about to learn that bitter lesson of taking things for granted when he walked away from God's protection and suffered the consequences.

They say that the wounds from a friend run deeper and hurt even more. Following that fateful night, Paul, wounded by many "*Friends*" over the coming months, faced the onslaught that commenced the night Paul opened his door to one of his closest friends whom Dark Forces had taken capture outside of his comprehension.

SAM

"It wasn't only his eyes, Sam, burning like red coals in his head, and it was what he or they said." Paul attempted to relate the night's event to his best friend, Sam, at the church the following day.

He hadn't slept the entire night, tossing and turning after his frightening ordeal, and had come down to the church at 6 am to prepare the communion effects for the Sunday Service, which took place at 11 am. It consisted of cutting the bread up into little cubes and filling the tiny glasses with fruit juice which would be handed around the congregation during the service at the time of communion. His friend, Sam, by providence, had come down early to fix a problem with one of the minibusses.

"What do you mean, "They? What happened? What's wrong?" Sam gripped Paul's shoulders as he searched his eyes for the answers.

Sam put a reassuring arm around him and drew a chair from under the kitchen table, "Take your time and tell me the whole story from start to finish."

He accepted the seat offered by Sam and, choking back the tears, began to relate the sinister events of the previous evening.

It all began just before midnight on Saturday, as he was in his study at the rear of the house, cutting the figures out for a flan- a-graph picture story he used to illustrate his Sunday school lesson the next day. He hadn't had time to prepare his work during the week and was now paying the price for his bad planning.

He thought to himself, *if you fail to plan, you plan to fail.*

In 1992, computerized overhead projectors were in their infancy. So, Paul used laminated sheets on an overhead projector to teach the songs and choruses to the children. But he needed something better than laminated sheets projected onto a screen to help bring his stories to life. No one could transform the bible stories in the way Paul told them.

The kids thought he was nuts, as he would enter the person's character in each presentation. The children would sit, captivated and google-eyed as his story unfolded. The other teachers and parents who were present thought *his lift did not go all the way to the top,* as he acted out the different parts and actions of the stories. But the kids loved it, nuts and all as he was.

The Flan a-graph had been an idea he had brought to Sam one day. Sam's ministry in the church included Sunday School Superintendent, youth leader, one of the minibus drivers, mechanics, and always on hand in an emergency. They say that 20% of the people of a church do 80% of the work. Sam was a significant part of that 20%. But he knew his ministry lay in having the heart of a servant and was an honest "Barnabas," encouraging everyone who needed a hand up or a hand around the shoulder.

When Paul spoke about his idea of using a flan a-graph and told Sam that he had ordered one and paid for it out of monies he had set aside for this work, his friend insisted on giving Paul half the cost of the materials. That was the nature of Sam. Since coming to the church in 1986, Sam and Paul had become close friends and brothers with the same plan, to reach as much of the town's youth for Jesus.

What was to become known in Northern Ireland as "The Troubles," which had started in late 1968 and would continue up to the signing of the Good Friday Agreement in 1998, had affected practically every citizen of Northern Ireland.

The IRA destroyed the entire country by planting their devices and bombs into businesses, shops, and supermarkets, creating terror and mayhem.

Shootings and killings were reported in the papers daily. High walls now separated Protestant and Catholic areas to keep them from killing each other. Hatred hung over the country like a wet blanket thrown over the embers of a fire, the smoke of grief and hopelessness stinging the eyes of those who watched the media reports of shootings and bombings every night.

Fear of the unknown is the fertilizer for hatred. Hatred fuelled by the fake news and bigotry already in place starts the battle. The battle had now turned into a bloody war. Sam and Paul both realized that there was only one way to bring peace to Northern Ireland. They would unite the youth, the future generation, of the towns together as followers of Jesus, whom Paul kept informing everyone was never either a Catholic or a Protestant. The message of hope and love would gradually spread throughout Ireland as these young boys and girls grew into mature loving adults.

The Sunday school had grown from 30 kids to over 150 excited, happy young people from both sides of the community. At the Sunday school prize-giving, the church entertained Catholic and Protestant parents, proud of their children's achievements. Some of them had never experienced a Pentecostal church service, filled with praise and worship, guitars, keyboards, fiddles, flutes, and drums, played by these young teenagers, as they worshipped God through their music.

Peter and Shirley Grower had become an integral part of that growing close-knit community because of their exceptional talent as singers and musicians. Peter, a sound engineer in a local recording studio, became interested in Paul's family as all the children were singers. He taught Paul's eldest son, Stephen, to play Bass and acoustic guitar and the techniques of running a sound desk. Stephen was now in charge of their equipment at all their concerts.

But that was all about to change dramatically under the direction of Evil.

"Oh Sam, those eyes burning into my brain and that horrible voice!" Paul was in convulsions.

"Calm down," consoled Sam, "From the beginning, slowly, Paul."

Paul taking a sip from the offered glass of water, started his narrative again from the knocking on the door.

"I brought them into my study for prayer. Shirley seemed to have Laryngitis, and she could only whisper. So, I sat the two of them down on the couch and knelt in front of them, taking Peter's hand and Shirley's hand and asking them to take each other's hand. I started to pray for Shirley.

I felt the room grow icy cold, so much so that I began to shiver. I first thought Peter then had started speaking in '*Other Tongues*,' but it was a horrible guttural tongue, sort of at the back of his throat. I was now shivering that much that my teeth began to chatter. Then suddenly, Shirley let out a piercing scream and jumped off the couch to the opposite wall. I had kept my eyes closed as I prayed, but I suddenly opened them, and Peter's eyes had turned into two blazing embers glaring at me as he tried to head-butt me, but his head kept bouncing off some barrier as if a clear screen was between the two of us.

I jumped back from him in shock, realizing that a demonic entity had materialized in the room, and, at that, Peter swiveled his legs around and started to levitate up off the couch. Shirley, who had amazingly recovered her voice, was screaming the house down over in the corner."

Sam's face had paled as he rose from his seat to attend to the boiling kettle.

"Take a breather, Paul, and a cup of warm tea."

In a minute, Paul had the warm mug between his hands and continued with his horror story as his friend took a gulp from his cup and sat down again, shivering slightly.

"I know nothing about demonology, Sam, but someone once told me that before casting a demon out, you must ask it its name to do so. I was also afraid that Shirley's screaming would wake the kids up and that the neighbors would phone the police on hearing the racket. So, I took a run, jumped onto Peter like a cowboy would mount a horse, and screamed at him,' What's your name?'.

I realize now that I should not have gone near him, but should have commanded, the spirit to leave in Jesus's Name. Without calling on God's protection, doing what I did only left me open for an attack.

The only response from him, or it was a horrible guttural voice,

"Never mind our name, we know your name, and you're F***ed. We will destroy you and your effing family, your effing job, your house, your marriage, your life. YOU'RE EFFING DEAD...! – DEAD...! - EFFING DEAD, MCGOWAN...! We have you".

Peter was ranting and foaming at the mouth. He threw me across the room as if I were a pillow onto the floor.

Just at that, my wife came through the door with two of the girls behind her. She immediately placed her hand on top of his forehead, saying,

'Be still in Jesus' Name,' and Peter dropped to the couch, woke up, shook his head, and said, 'What happened?'

Shirley, by this time, was quivering on her knees on the floor, repeating, 'Stay away from me. Stay away from me.'

I was shaking with I don't know what – fright – anger - disbelief – horror? It was like I had awakened from a sinister nightmare. I couldn't stop shaking, Sam. I'm still shaking. What am I going to do? What can I do? That thing is going to kill me and destroy my family".

"Calm down! Calm down, Paul! Nothing can harm you or your family" Sam tried to reason with him, "God will protect you and your family."

"Then how did that thing get into my home? You weren't there. You didn't hear it, and you didn't see it. Don't tell me it won't harm me. It already has."

"Look, Paul, get yourself up home. I'll finish this job up for you here. Also, you won't be driving any minibus today. Just bring your family to church later, and I will figure out how to tackle this problem". Sam led Paul out the door of the church and as far as his car where he suddenly stopped,

"I have it! I know who can help us - and to build your faith and show you how the supernatural works, I will not tell you his name, nor am I going to approach him about this. I will pray about this whole business, and I guarantee that this person will approach you after church. Just trust me on this, Paul".

"Stop playing games Sam. Can't you see that I am at my wit's end?" retorted Paul.

"And you will always find God at Wit's End," was Sam's rebuttal, as he rapped the roof of the car and closed the door after Paul. "See you after church. Have faith, Brother."

Paul headed back home feeling a little bit better after the God-ordained meeting with his ever faithful and true friend, Sam, and wondered how God would fix this. However, fate and the dark forces that had entered his life had other plans for Paul.

The Battle Begins

The service that morning seemed surreal as Paul prayed that it was all a nightmare from which he would soon awake, but his thoughts kept continually drifting in and out of the previous evening's horrific events. Despite all of his pleadings, the heavens were silent. After the service, he carried the empty cruets from the sanctuary to the kitchen in a daze. He shivered, even in the warmth of the church. His thoughts at the sink were interrupted as the kitchen door slowly opened.

Norm stood in the doorway of the kitchen, scratching his bald head. The church elder seemed confused.

"Hi, Norm, I never saw you come in. Is everything alright?" Paul was washing out the communion vessels at the sink.

"I must be losing it, Paul. I was at the front door speaking to the folk as they left, and I thought that I heard the Lord say, 'Go down and see Paul.' Sorry to disturb you, Brother. I'm losing it." Norm turned to leave.

"No, Norm, you're not. Has Sam been speaking to you - ABOUT ME?"

"No, I spoke with him this morning, but he never mentioned you. Why? What's up?" queried the church elder.

"Norm, do you have any experience in exorcism?"

"Aha!" exclaimed Norm, so that's your trouble, is it?"

"No, Norm! It's not my trouble, and I want nothing to do with it." Paul could feel the tears welling up in his eyes as his voice broke off into a whimper.

"So," quizzed Norm, "It's someone else's trouble, and you want nothing to do with it. Paul, the only thing you will get sitting on the fence are splinters in your backside."

Paul burst into uncontrollable floods of tears.

"Oh, Paul! Dear God, what has happened to you, man?" Norm ran to him and held him in a bear hug, "Tell me the story, son."

Paul blurted out the events of the previous night choking back the tears,

"I'm so frightened, Norm, for my family, my home, my job. That demon said it would take them all and kill me. I couldn't sleep the entire night. I don't think I'll ever sleep-those horrible eyes – that face," Paul was in convulsions now.

"Paul, son, sit down here" Norm pulled a chair from under the table, "I've dealt with this stuff before. I'm so glad I came down on the prompting from the Lord. Does that not show you that He's got this?" Norm poured him a glass of water and threw some blackberry juice into it, "Here, swallow this. Are you able to teach your Sunday School class today, or will I get someone to cover for you?"

"I'll be alright, thanks, Norm" Paul wiped his face with his handkerchief.

"Right, obviously Sam knows about this because you asked me if he said anything. Sam, you, and I will visit the Grower home this afternoon when you finish up. Collect me on your way. Don't worry. We can sort this out with God's help."

Unfortunately for Paul McGowan, it would be many years, and immeasurable damage would occur before it would eventually be 'Sorted.'

Sam and Paul collected Norm around 4:30 pm. He had brought anointing oil and his tattered old bible.

Shirley answered the door, "Peter's up in the bathroom, and he'll be down in a minute. We are just home from Ulster Hall. It went well, and I was wondering if......."

Shirley burst into uncontrollable sobs as she buried her face in her hands, turning her back on the group.

Norm reached out and held her. "Don't worry, Pet. We are here to sort this".

Sort it out? Paul shivered.

Peter entered the room, "I'm sorry you were bothered, Lads. Shirley should not have called you."

"She didn't, Peter. Please, take a seat. I said, '**Sit down, Peter!**'"

Paul was a bit taken aback by the tone of Norm's voice.

"We are first of all going to pray, and then I will anoint the house. Then, Peter, you and I will have a chat out in the garden," Norm glared at Peter.

Peter's face paled as he sat down in a corner armchair.

13

Norm prayed softly. Then he proceeded to anoint the doorposts and lintels of each of the rooms downstairs, "Nothing out of the ordinary down here. May we go upstairs, and I'll lead the way."

Norm stopped so suddenly at the top of the stairs that Shirley fell against him, "What's the room at the end of the landing used for" Norm stretched his arm in the direction of the closed door at the end of the landing.

"That's our little daughter's room," Shirley replied.

"Downstairs now, you guys, I have work to do. Do not come up these stairs no matter what you hear, and I am protected."

Paul had walked as far as the bottom step of the staircase. As he heard Norm's specific instruction, a feeling of dread began to rise in the pit of his stomach.

What's going on in that room? Will Norm be safe? He felt a bit of a coward but could not face a sequel to the previous evening. *Hopefully, Norm **will** sort it.*

Paul turned around in relief at the bottom of the stairs and went back into the lounge. Finding Peter there with his face buried in his hands, Paul sat at the room's far end. The others had gone to the kitchen.

"What am I going to do?" cried Peter.

"I don't know, Peter. Norm said he'd sort it."

"He can't sort it. I cannot remember a thing about last night, and Shirley won't come near me," Peter began to cry uncontrollably, "What's happening to me?"

"I'll get you some tea, Peter." Paul rose and went to the kitchen, where Sam and Shirley spoke in hushed voices.

They stopped as Paul entered, "How's Peter?" Sam looked up at Paul.

"He's in a bad way," said Paul reaching for the kettle. I'll make him some tea. Sit where you are, Shirley love. You've been through the mill."

When Paul returned with the tea five minutes later, Norm and Peter were in a heated conversation,

"Be with you in a minute, Paul. Leave Peter's tea there on the table. See you shortly; you and Sam go out to the car and wait for me."

Norm looked very concerned, possibly angry.

Paul was looking across at Peter's white face, and it looked as if Norm had been lecturing him. He left the room still with the cup and saucer clenched in his hand.

"Come on, Sam, we've got to leave. Norm will be out in a minute."

"Don't leave me," whimpered Shirley.

"It's OK, love," consoled Sam, "I'll ask Norm to speak with you before he goes. See you out in the car in a moment, Paul."

Sam put his hand on Paul's shoulder as they walked into the hall, "I didn't hear him come down. Did you find out what happened in the room?"

"No, Sam, but he is angry with Peter about something. I don't know what?"

All sorts of thoughts were going through Paul's addled brain, ideas that he prayed would not be true, as he tried to brush them out of his head without success.

As paul went out to the car, Sam entered the lounge to speak with Norm and Peter. They came out to the car a half-hour later, both of them drained and exhausted.

"What happened?" Paul asked, on edge now.

"Serious situation, Son. Drive," ordered Norm, "We need to form a prayer group, Sam, to cover Paul and his Family and the Grower Family, and we will not inform the Pastor."

"Why not, Norm?" queried Paul into the rear-view mirror.

"Never mind, Paul, just follow my lead on this." Norm tapped Paul's shoulder.

"Ron, the treasurer is a sound man, and Pastor Denis won't say anything if you ask him," said Sam.

"Are you sure, Sam? This situation must have a lid on it."

"I'm sure Norm, two sound Men of God," replied Sam.

Norm was deep in thought, "OK, Sam, now not a word to Bobby Millar, right, Guys. He will only do his nut over this and need not be informed."

The relationship between the Senior Pastor, Bobby Millar, and Paul had been on a knife-edge for some time. Bobby rang Paul, who was working in the local estate agency in town and asked him to put a factory building up for sale at the rear of the church. The building had been bequeathed to the church in a will many years ago.

"We need the money. The new church project has run over budget", declared the Pastor to Paul's query.

"I don't believe that's your decision, and that is a matter for the Oversight to discuss." Paul was surprised at this sudden note of authority in his voice.

"How dare you. I'm the Pastor of this church," Bobby Millar fumed.

"And I'm a Deacon, and I'm calling a meeting," Paul retorted.

Pastor Millar slammed the phone down.

Didn't realize that those guys lost their temper, thought Paul to himself.

*****

"Paul, have you a word from the Lord on this?" Norm inquired at the oversight meeting.

"No," answered Paul, "Just using my head. We will need that building for the youth as this church grows, and I am positive that we will eventually own the complete block, including that drinking club at the corner."

"We cannot get planning permission to use that factory building for anything. It's just a large vacant garage and store" the Pastor glared across his desk at Paul.

Walter spoke up, "We could erect a wooden structure inside it, Pastor. We don't need planning for that."

"Brilliant!" answered Sam, "We have all the tradesmen we need in the church. I'll get started on our new youth building".

"We're over budget as it is, Sam," moaned the Pastor.

"I didn't ask you for any of the budgets, Pastor," was Sam's rebuttal, "I propose we don't sell the property, Brothers."

"I second that," replied Norm.

Paul was straight away on Bobby Millar's naughty list, and it wasn't even Christmas.

Paul's words would bear fruit many years later, but this was now, and tensions were high.

"This is not over yet." Roared the Pastor as he walked out of the meeting.

"Don't worry, Paul," said Walter, "He'll soon cool off."

But Bobby Millar was a Businessman, and he would ensure that no one would dare interfere in his business.

Later that particular evening, Paul received a phone call,

"Hello Paul, it's Agnes."

Agnes was a prophet who gave encouraging words to the congregation at the Sunday meetings.

"I don't know if you heard or know. Bobby Millar has silenced me, so I have left that Church. I just rang you with a warning. Be very careful, Paul. You are about to enter the battle of your life. I am praying for you."

"Poor woman! She's lost it," thought Paul as he hung up the phone.

However, Paul could not stop thinking of Agnes's dire warning over the next few nights.

Memories of various events involving Bobby Millar seemed to consider anyone rising above the crowd within the assembly as a threat to his position of authority.

Paul tried to shrug it off, but the thoughts prevailed enough for him to try to pray for forgiveness. He was also still upset because his pastor had stayed away from his mother's funeral, and that hurt.

Was it because it was in a Roman Catholic Chapel? Was he worried about what people would say or think?

He was devastated to find his mother dead on Mother's Day, 1989. He felt a sudden uneasiness the Friday before and mentioned to his wife that he had a concern for her,

"Maybe we could drop her Mother's-day plant around early."

"No, we have too much to do without visiting your mum, and she has no phone. We will waste time going all the way over, and she may be out. Wait until Sunday when you collect her for dinner," argued Lesley, Paul's wife.

He was numb and full of remorse that he had not called to see his dear Mum that Friday.

His Pastor never showed up at the local Chapel for the first service in the North, but his friends and assistant pastor Denis did.

His Mother was then transported to County Mayo and buried near her home.

It rained throughout the five-hour journey to Rossport, where over a hundred people had been standing in the rain for almost two hours outside the chapel. Funny thing, the Sun came out like a beautiful summer's day during the entire ceremony around the graveside, and then the clouds burst open as soon as it finished.

Paul discovered that his mother had been praying for him throughout his life, only after she died, and he again suffered the deep sorrow and regret of her passing. He found the note in her handbag days after her funeral in an old stained brown envelope with his name written on it in his mother's copperplate handwriting.

"Dearest Paul,

I have prayed for you all of my life, every precious day, Our Lord has granted me on this earth, since ever you were my wee boy. I have asked Him to Bless & Protect you and your precious family, and I know that he has and will because He has never once let me down, and He won't let you down.

If you are reading this, I am with Him now, and I will continue to ask Him to look after you. I love you dearly, my precious son, and always will. I will see you again when you reach the home which He has prepared for you over here.

All my love, forever, Mam. X.

Paul's tears were uncontrollable.

*****

THE ANSWERED PRAYER

"You're not taking that promotion, Paul. I don't care if they are making you a director. When Bert gave you that job, he said he'd make you a partner, and then he sold the darn business to that blasted consortium" Lesley, Paul's wife, was off on one.

"Stop it, honey. Bert has been more than reasonable to us. My salary increased immediately when the changeover occurred. Bert negotiated that and the new car, plus a pension. Now they have agreed to give me a new BMW, a luxurious office in the center of Belfast, plus an extra ten grand a year. What are you on about?

"I'll tell you, '*What I am on about.*' The IRA are blowing Belfast to bits, and you are moving into a Glass Cage behind the City Hall. If a bomb goes off anywhere near that place, never mind probably planted in it, I have lost my husband, and our children have lost their Dad. No BMW nor any amount of 'Filthy Lucre' is worth that!" Lesley was upset and worried, "Remember, you could have lost your life that time your new van was hi-jacked, and they used it to blow up Franklin street around the corner from that new office. Don't test Providence."

Paul had long forgotten those incidents which were suddenly blazoned across his mind, like a movie on a big screen. He found himself shuddering at that horrendous period of his early marriage to the girl of his dreams which were to be relived much later by the dark, cold waters of the lakes just a few miles from his home.

But for now, thoughts were re-emerging back to his early career in the haulage industry. He had just taken delivery of his second brand new transit, and he had loaded it with the day's deliveries for Avon Cosmetics to some of their agents in Belfast.

The IRA hijacked the van, stole the load from it, planted a two thousand-pound bomb inside it, and blew up the whole of Franklin Street in the center of Belfast City, destroying everything in the block.

The Police later informed him that they probably hijacked his vehicle because they would have been watching the vans that delivered and collected goods from the suppliers in Franklin Street, and all of them were Paul's customers. So, his van would not have been considered 'Suspicious' by the army.

Shortly after starting their delivery business, Paul and Lesley had bought a house in Stranmillis Gardens when they married in 1970. It was one of the better areas of Belfast near the University. There should not have been any trouble from rioters, bombs, or civil unrest.

One early morning two men on a motorbike drew up outside Jim Gibson's grocery shop and shot him dead in front of his wife and children because he was a Roman Catholic. The following week another shopkeeper was shot two streets away for the same reason, the gunman shouting 'Taigs Out,' as he ran away. Then a Catholic High Court Judge was murdered at a Catholic Church on the Malone Road coming out of Mass. The police warned Paul that Roman Catholic Businesspeople in the area were the targets and it would be wise to move. He took the advice and moved to Ballyclare.

Maybe Lesley's instinct was right. But what could he do? He had accepted the offer from his Managing Director and was to take up his new position in Belfast on the following Monday.

Paul had never seen his wife so upset, "Well," she continued, "I am jolly well getting to prayer, and the Lord will hand you a better job - on a plate in this here town. Stick that in your wallet."

"Well, He'd better hurry up. I have accepted the position and move in on Monday."

Paul left the house in a sour mood to drive to the lakes, intending to go for a long walk to calm himself down after the haranguing match, "Better to live on a flat roof than in the house of a nagging woman," he misquoted the Bible.

The phone in his car rang, "Hello Paul, William Stevens here. Have you got a minute?"

 "Yes, go ahead, William. How can I help you?"

"Can we meet for lunch tomorrow? I have an important deal I would like to discuss with you?"

"Sure. One pm is fine, William. See you in the Garden Restaurant."

A Finance House looking for money from me? It must be a massive commercial mortgage. Great, I can't wait to meet him, and I can't wait to shove that under the wife's neb.

Paul smiled, changed his mind and his mood, and drove home.

Lesley met him on her way down the stairs as he came in, "I prayed about that Job, by the way, Paul, and you will hear about it this week. Do what you feel you should do, but not without praying before you make your final decision, for I know God will answer my prayer, and I also know that only He can direct you to the right decision."

"I'm sorry, Love, I've already made my decision, and William Stevens is giving me a big commercial mortgage to start me off on Monday," Paul smirked unkindly with a headmaster inflection in his voice.

"It's not over until the Fat Lady Sings," fired back his wife from the kitchen.

*****

"What? What do you mean a 'Bank Manager'? Are you offering me a job as a Bank Manager? I don't know the first thing about banking, William." The offer had taken Paul totally by surprise.

William Stevens, the Managing Director of one of the oldest established Finance Houses in Northern Ireland, went straight to the point as he sat down.

"You know enough. You're doing commercial loans to beat the band. I have had my eye on you since you took over the financial services for Bert, a perfect friend of mine who never stops singing your praises.

I recently met Bill Webb from the Progressive Building Society on some business, who said that an idea of yours had made them a fortune. You told them to change their Articles of Memorandum & Association to facilitate Commercial Lending, and your builder clients are borrowing development money from them a 5% above the domestic rate. You persuaded him to lend building development loans by offering an office on every house building site to promote Progressive Building Society Mortgages. Ingenious! How did you come up with that one?

I have also heard on good authority that you borrow money from Norwich Union's Fire fund at 4% above the gilt rate of 2%, and the banks charge 21%." William had a large file containing Paul's CV. *Where did he get all this stuff on me?* wondered Paul.

"Yes, Paul, you know enough about Banking for me to offer you the position of General Manager, plus the fact that we have just this week purchased a Financial services Brokerage beside us, and I want you to run that as well.

So, you will inherit the position and the credentials of a Bank Manager since we have a proper Banking Licence, which should look very well on your CV. "By the way," smiled William, "you won't be required to do any of the Banking Exams. Eat up and enjoy your lunch and the promotion. You're buying the next one."

That darned wife of mine and her prayers thought Paul; *the Company will go ballistic.*

*****

26

The earned commissions in the brokerage alone during the first six months amounted to over £140,000. Paul was back in the cut and thrust of the business he loved, now satisfied that he had made the right choice, but also had once again placed his feet squarely on the slippery slope of Egotism and Pride that comes before a fall.

William requested him to take over his boss's duties by attending the monthly 'Banking Federation Meetings' at the exclusive Reform Club in Royal Avenue in the center of Belfast. He quickly made friends with all the heads of the Banking Community in Northern Ireland. When Quinton Hogg took him under his wing and helped him along in his new career, with tips on commercial banking and with some of the more complex cases that landed on Paul's desk, his knowledge grew exponentially. Eventually, Quinton proposed him for full membership of the exclusive Reform Club. That was the door to Satan's trap and the first nail in Paul's coffin.

The Devil is very subtle. He is happy to bide his time one bite at a time as he slowly sucks you into his swamp until you're his.

Paul had now decided that the Reform Club would be the venue where he would entertain all of his clientele from then on, silver service, al-a-carte menu, best of wines, no women allowed – except in the private rooms – but that would come later. For now, the ambiance and 5-star dining, smack dab in the middle of the City would adequately suffice for now.

So began Paul's dual life and confirmation of the adage, 'Good living for a living.' God abhors two-faced people and double standards. So, allowed this disobedient sheep to wander off down the road and into Satan's Territory. Free will is a two-edged sword, and Paul had now boarded the runaway train headed for disaster.

Hence the state of play the night the Devil knocked on Paul's door in the person of his best friend, after he had accused Paul of his two-faced way of life before the Throne of Grace and pleaded his case in the Courts of heaven, for control of Paul's life. Satan still has the power to come into that court, as he did with Job, but instead, Job obeyed God, Paul did not.

THE SCREW BEGINS TO TURN

The phone rang on Paul's office desk as he opened his door. "Let me get my coat off for pity's sake, woman." He answered the phone, "'Yes, Madge?"

"There is a Pastor Millar on the line, and he says it's urgent. Are you able to take his call at present?"

What the heck does he want now. I'm in enough of a state without him bothering me, thought Paul, "Put him through, Madge,"

"Yes, Pastor, how can I help you?"

"I need to discuss an urgent matter with you immediately. Can you come around to my home straight away?" Bobby Millar sounded stressed.

"I'll meet you at the church, Pastor. It's nearer to my office".

"At my home **now**, Paul," the Pastor slammed his phone down."

"Ignorant Cretin of a man!" muttered Paul, who had a hectic day lined up.

He rang his boss, "William, I have to go out on some urgent business. Do you mind taking my calls until I return?"

"Go ahead, Paul. I'll take care of anything urgent, and your secretary can look after the rest." "By the way, can you call

29

in with me on the way back? We have been forced to make a few changes in our administration, and I need to advise you and ask for your advice. Come in and see me immediately you return, Paul, and we can go out and discuss this privately over coffee with my directors. Thanks."

*****

"I believe you cast a demon out of Peter Grower." Bobby Millar was drumming his fingers on his black oak desk's immaculately polished glass top.

"I cast nothing out of anyone. What are you getting at?"

"Don't' lie to me. Peter was here early this morning in a very agitated state. What have you done or said to him?"

The Pastor did not seem to grasp the seriousness of the situation, nor did he even try to understand that Peter was in grave danger and needed expert help. He appeared to be more concerned about the story reaching the public domain. Paul suddenly realized a cover-up was hatching. The good name of his church was now at risk. They would ship Peter to some of the Pastor's USA colleagues. How was that going to help Peter and Shirley's dire situation?

"Well, if he was here, you already have the story. I need not waste any more of our time elaborating on it," Paul turned to leave.

"I want to know what happened. Take a seat," the indignant Pastor replied.

Funny how this seat is somewhat lower than his seat? Thought Paul as he angrily obeyed the command.

"Tell me the Truth!" the pastor thumped his desk.

"The truth is that Norm, Sam, and I...."

"NORM AND SAM know about this? Who else have you told? Are you trying to wreck this Church?" Bobby Millar became belligerent.

Paul could feel his face starting to blush with anger, "Are you more interested in your Church or the People of 'Your Church'?" he fired at the Pastor, "Pastor Denis and Ron, the treasurer know as well because we have formed a prayer group."

"On who's authority? Why wasn't I consulted about this? You are silenced with immediate effect on this matter and will take nothing more to do with Peter & Shirley Grower, and I'll sort this 'Prayer Meeting.' If this gets out, the church is gone."

Paul felt the anger begin to rise in him as the purple-faced pastor ranted on, "I'm leaving before I say something I regret,"

He pushed his chair back and walked to the door.

"Come back here. I haven't finished," roared the voice behind the desk.

"I have!" Paul slammed the door of the Pastor's study on purpose.

Mrs. Millar met him in the hallway, "O dear, Pastor sounds very upset."

"Not as upset as I am, Mrs. Millar. Goodbye." Paul left, trying to keep his temper.

As he drove back to the office, he suddenly realized that Bobby Millar had delayed him longer than he had anticipated, "Has the Boss gone out, Madge?"

"He had a very urgent appointment with the directors of the bank, Paul. He was hoping that you could have accompanied him."

Paul was much later to find out just how serious that meeting had been and how Paul could have saved the company from disaster. But he missed the meeting.

"Oh, grief. Why didn't you tell me about this?"

"He told me not to say anything, but he asked me this morning if you had an hour free, and I said yes. He looked distraught, Paul. I hope everything is all right." Madge looked very upset.

Paul did not see William the rest of the week. He had gone off on urgent business, leaving a taped message for Paul and the Office Manager to look after things until his return.

That Friday, as Paul drew up into the office car park, he noticed a large furniture van at the front door and two uniformed police officers talking with two suits outside the front door. *What on earth is going on?* he wondered as he locked the car door.

One of the officers and a suit approached him, "You are?" queried the Suit.

"What's up, Gentlemen? I'm the General Manager, Paul McGowan."

The police officer spoke first, "Sorry Mr. McGowan, your premises have been closed. These men are from the enforcement of Judgements office and are removing all the chattels belonging to the company."

"And you may leave that car here as well," said the suit as he handed Paul the warrant, "You may go up to the employment exchange and sign on. That's where your staff has been sent."

"And you may go to Hell," replied Paul, "How? What? What is going on here? Where's the Boss? Our company is making thousands."

"Your parent company is not, and that is the actual problem. You, as General Manager of both, should have been aware of this situation, and I'm afraid that I must do my job."

"I don't know about all of this, sir," added the constable, "We are just here to make sure these men are not interfered with doing their job. Do you know where the exchange is?

"Yes, I damn well do" Paul got back into the car, ignoring the instructions of the Bailiff, and drove to the exchange.

"Sorry to hear the shocking news, Mr. McGowan. One of the oldest businesses in the town gone bankrupt", the counter clerk appeared at first sympathetic

"What do you mean, 'Bankrupt.' We were making big profits."

"Yes, but your parent company wasn't. They were out repossessing £500 suites of furniture and selling them cheap in the auctions. You're the General Manager, and surely you knew all this."

I hadn't anything to do with that end of the finance operation, and the Retail Section handled that business, not me."

"Well, if people could not have afforded the excessive payment plan, they should have been declined by your office and made another arrangement with the shops. Your finance house with your high rates of interest puts people in trouble," the guy looked as though he was pleased about the demise of the company.

"The mortgage rate is sky-high, and people are in financial difficulties," Paul walked out in disgust.

A week later, he received a letter saying that he would not be receiving unemployment benefits until he was means-tested. The department would not now be able to pay his interest-only mortgage.

He phoned William, the poor man who had lost the Family Business, and was blaming his own wrong decisions for what had happened,

"I'm sorry, Paul, I should have waited for you and brought you to that meeting. The Bank explained that they could help me, and I foolishly believed their lies. The Parent Company had an agreed overdraft limit of £1 Million, and it had slowly grown to £1.5 million. Many customers had stopped paying, and we needed cash flow to keep the business afloat until the mortgage rate decreased. We had a book worth a value of £3 Million. The bank told me that they would organize a buyer for it.

The offer was £1 Million. The bank told me to accept the offer and start again, and that would give me breathing space. The agreed sale took place. With funds paid, they called in the

£500,000. The company who bought our book was a subsidiary of the bank."

Paul called up to the petrol station to explain what had happened to the company.

"I'm ringing the police, or else you can pay me. You're the Boss," the garage owner, an ex- B-Special, (*part-time police force hated by the Nationalist community in Northern Ireland*), screamed at Paul from behind his counter.

"I'm not the boss, but I will pay my car's petrol account when I get sorted, but you will have to pursue the rest through the receiver," Paul tried to calm him.

"I'm phoning the cops."

"It's not a police matter, and it's a civil matter" Paul was losing his patience.

"We'll see about that. These cops won't be civil to you when they meet you. I know where you live, you Fenian Bastard!" The B-Special eyeballed Paul.

That was it. Paul lost his temper, "I'm no Fenian, you trumped-up Black B-Special. Well, you can chase the receiver for everything now." He jumped into the car and drove off.

The following day two detectives arrived at Paul's door demanding payment for the garage account. Paul asked for a warrant card to prove they were who they said they were, wrote down the details, and told them he was reporting them for illegal debt collecting. They immediately arrested him for driving off without paying, threw him in a cell for the rest of the day, and did not come near him. At 7 pm, Pastor Denis arrived with Paul's solicitor and bailed him out.

"Bert heard about this from Pastor Denis. Your wife rang Denis. Bert has paid your account. I dropped the cheque up to the garage. By the way, did you threaten the arresting officers with intent, Paul?" The solicitor asked.

"No, I told them that I was reporting them for debt collecting and using threatening behavior. I informed the two detectives that my cousin was a Chief Superintendant in Strand Road." Paul allowed himself to smirk for a moment.

"That was rather unfortunate. The police officers must make this official to save their skins and have charged you with Fraud. They have the law on their side and will take the case to trial. It won't stick, but it may save their jobs," countered the lawyer.

"But I am innocent," argued Paul.

"It will still go to court and will probably hit the papers," the solicitor warned.

"Been there before and beat them. God won't let this happen" Paul was a bit over-confident, but he remembered the last court appearance where God had saved his skin. He repeated the experience to his two friends.

*****

It was a year earlier.

Paul had rung his friend, Jim, to see if he could improve the taste of the coffee from the machine that he had supplied. "The water's your problem, Paul, not the machine. I'll call in this afternoon and explain what chlorine does to coffee and tea".

Later that day, the guy walked into Paul's office with a water filter under his arm. "Try that water," he poured a paper cup of water out for Paul.

Paul tasted the offered cup, "That water is delicious, Jim."

"I took that water out of your tap, but I have filtered it before giving it to you," said Jim.

"Your joking? How much does that filter cost."

"A lot. How would you like one for free?" Jim then pulled a photocopied cheque out of his jacket, "That is one of my distributors. All he does is let people taste that water, and they order a filter, and I fit it. He made £10,000 last month."

"What!" exclaimed Paul, "How?"

Jim smiled, "Paul just do what he does. You have a sales team here, and your company makes a profit on the insurance policies your reps sell. Recruit a few part-timers to flog these water filters and make yourself a healthy second income."

Paul was so successful that the filter company requested that he register for VAT within two months because his turnover had reached the VAT threshold.

Paul duly registered, not realizing that the commissions would now carry a VAT content on the self-invoicing system that the company used, as they did not require invoices from their distributors.

Paul then paid commission to his people without checking if they had registered for VAT. That commission included a portion of the rebated VAT to Paul.

Two men from Customs arrived at his home. Customs & Excise have the power to enter any premises without a warrant. "We need to audit your books. Where do you keep your office paperwork? We already have the company records pertinent to your sales, which are fairly sizeable".

Three days later, Paul received a bill from the VAT Office for a sum three times the amount he figured that he owed.

He then received a summons to appear in court. He worried so much about his dilemma that it sent his blood pressure dangerously high, and his doctor told him to pack the business in and prescribed medication for hypertension.

Paul knew that the answer to his problem could only be found on his knees.

He received the instructions in that position, as a voice spoke straight to his heart "Don't take the oath on the stand."

He rang his previous Pastor at AOG, Bethshan Tabernacle in Belfast, "Bob, I'm in court tomorrow, and I feel the Lord telling me not to take the oath."

"Well, yes, I understand what you mean, Paul, 'Let your yay be yay, and your nay be nay," but you are not doing any harm swearing an oath in court, as long as you tell the truth," the helpful pastor replied.

"I will always do that anyway, Pastor."

"Well, the only advice that I can give you, Paul, is if you are certain that God has laid that on your heart, do that, trust Him to do the rest, and promise to tell the truth in court. Let us pray about it now, Paul, and go into that court with God," The pastor blessed Paul and hung up.

*****

"Ronnie, I'm not taking the oath," he informed his accountant on the courtroom steps.

"Now, Paul, you are in enough trouble as it is. You could be in contempt of court if you refuse to take the oath. I have the true figures here, and they show a different lower amount than charged. We can make a deal to pay any debt off, and you don't mess with these people," Paul's accountant tried to reason with him.

"I'm not taking the Oath, Ronnie. I've prayed, and God told me not to," Paul was adamant.

"Your nuts. God doesn't talk to people. I will not represent you if you go against the Court and the VAT office, and I have a reputation to uphold," Ronnie stuffed the file into his briefcase.

"Uphold it then. My Father God will uphold mine." That was that!

Paul took the stand. There were three men on the bench, which made Paul wonder.

"Take the Book in your right hand and read the card in front of you." The man in the middle spoke.

"Sorry, Your Honour, I'm a 'Born Again' Believer, and this book is precious to me, and I cannot take the oath." At that, Paul burst into tears.

"Mr. McGowan, calm yourself, sit down. Get the gentleman a glass of water. You're fine, Mr. McGowan, you do realize that you may affirm, but the penalty for perjury will still apply? Take a sip of that water and relax. We only want the truth on this matter."

The word 'Truth' rang in Paul's heart like a chapel bell. He reached into his pocket for one of his blood-pressure tablets.

"Are you on medication, Mr. McGowan? Would you pass those to the clerk of the court, please? I'd like to see them before we proceed."

The Judge examined the labels, "Trandate and Tenormin! These are very high doses. What was your last reading?"

"180 Over 120, your honor," Paul replied.

"What! You're a walking corpse, man. Do you owe this money?"

"No, but…." Paul stammered.

"Never mind the 'But,' do you owe this money?"

"No, Sir."

"That's better," replied the judge.

"The man says he doesn't owe this debt. How did you arrive at this figure?" He directed the question to the two men and the solicitor at the opposite table.

"We did an audit on his bank statements, your Honor."

"You did what? You did an audit on his bank accounts, did you?" there was a bit of a whispered discussion amongst the three men on the stand, "Do you see the state you have this man in. We wish to see you in chambers after court, gentlemen. Case dismissed. You may go, Mr. McGowan."

"But how much do I need to pay them, Sir."

"Nothing. I said case dismissed, and I apologize for the trouble caused to you in bringing you in front of this court. I hope you recover soon. Have a good day, Mr. McGowan".

Ronnie was on the steps of the court shaking his head and muttering away to himself as he looked at Paul's accounts, "All that work for nothing, and you get off with an apology? You've nearly persuaded me to join your church, Paul. I have never seen the likes of that in all my career".

Paul rang Bob Edgar in Bethshan to let him know the outcome, "Who was the Judge?"

Paul gave him the name, and Bob broke into peals of laughter, "He is a Believer, and I know him well. That affirmation the Lord advised you on was all it took. After all, Lord Jesus is an advocate for us with the Father, and an old VAT Court will not be a problem for Him. Thanks, Paul, you have increased my Faith a hundred-fold."

"What a story, man?" said the solicitor as they parted company, "You've nothing to worry about anyway, Paul. You have a direct line to the Man above."

*****

41

It didn't take Bobby Millar long to pick up the news of Paul's arrest

"I believe the RUC has charged you with fraud. You may resign from the oversight and step down from your ministries within the church until this matter has cleared up. That will also include Sunday School."

"Pastor, I will go before the church assembly and explain to them what happened."

"I'll say what you'll do in this church. By the way, you will still have a Ministry within this church", stated the Pastor, as he picked the fluff off Paul's lapel.

"What's that?" asked Paul.

"You may still clean it," was the curt reply.

Paul exploded, "And you can stick your blasted church and your god. I am out of here permanent."

"I've not finished yet," argued Bobby Millar.

"I am. Good Day, Sir."

Paul's mortgage started to run into arrears. He could not obtain a job in the Financial Services industry because of the impending fraud case. He took a sales job selling chemicals, but the competition was tough, and sales on commission only barely fed the family. He had started drinking again to help ease his worries, but that alienated his wife and made things even harder. He couldn't or wouldn't seek God to sort his problems as he kept believing his next deal was at the next call and remained in his stubborn "Sorry for himself" frame of mind.

After some months, he had still unsuccessfully tried to sell his home, and the lender repossessed it.

His job was gone, and his house was gone. His wife had threatened to pack his bags if he didn't stop drinking. His Church, and (*as he thought*), his God had also abandoned him. He had reached his limit.

That night Paul went to three pubs after hatching a plan to get drunk and end his life.

That was the night the Angel appeared to him at the Lakeside.

The Lake of Darkness & Dreams.

Paul stared unsteadily into the dark depths of the lake. The sound of the waters lapping off the side of the pier beckoning him closer. He thought he saw a face, looking up at him from the depths of the black lake in the light of the full moon, or was it the yellow sodium lamps reflecting their light from the council office's car park on the other side of the dark, gloomy waters.

"Joa-ump, Joa-ump, Joa-ump," the voice reverberated slowly in his head.

He looked closer at the face in the water. He seemed to have a horrible memory of it engulfing his brain fogged memory; *Was that a reflection of his face or was it another face?* He was too drunk even to care,

OK, I'm jumping in. The water's deep, and I'm too drunk to feel the cold; Paul had been to three bars that night and thrown out of the last two. But he didn't care anymore, and he was numb with either the cold or the drink.

He staggered back along the pier, then, with all the strength left in his now shaking body, he ran towards the edge of the dock and launched himself into the air.

'**Whump,**' a colossal hand or a fist, or something, collided with his chest knocking him sideways into the shrubbery. He lay there, in the damp bushes, catching his breath, too drunk to realize what had just happened.

"I didn't even see that branch in the dark," he slurred as he struggled back onto his feet again and staggered back up the pier for another erratic run towards the lake.

'Whump,' it was in the groin this time, and that one hurt severely as the back of his head hit the pavement. He felt the back of his aching head. He could not see what was on his hand in the darkness, but it smelt like blood.

He swore softly. "Yea, you were going to kill me. Well, now's your effing chance," he declared violently at the yellow face grinning up at him from the black, yellow illuminated water that he had just crawled over to on his hands and knees.

The yellow face rose nearer to the surface, still grinning. Paul recognized the face from that night in his home.

"Come on, you cowardly piece of filth. You've got me this time. You've got me 'Noowww'!"

Paul suddenly jumped off the pier.

'Whump, Whump,' he was catapulted into a large bush and was knocked unconscious this time.

He didn't know how long he lay there in a drunken daze, but through his flickering eyelids, he saw a pinprick of light. It seemed to be traveling slowly towards him, revolving and pulsing.

Now I'm seeing stars. Paul tried to focus his intoxicated eyes. *Maybe this is a dream, no, a nightmare,*

"Wake up, Paul, wake up, damn you."

But he didn't wake up, and the light traveled nearer and grew more prominent.

It had become an orb now, spinning in front of him. He shut his eyes tight, but he could still see the spinning sphere through his tightly closed eyelids.

Suddenly, and with a jerk, he was out of his body, floating above the ground moving higher, higher, above the yellow flickering lights upon the water.

A voice spoke to him, not audibly, more inside of him like a knowing, a telepathic communication,

"My child, if you die this night, this would be your judgment call. Consider it a life review. You have cursed God, but you have not died because the Almighty has not cursed you."

The voice in his soul continued,

"You will find the thread of time connecting with Heaven's governance in the moments of the upcoming confluence on your path as that power influences the cosmic forces which protect you upon your planned journey through this life.

Consider times and seasons the help of the Almighty was available in your past life and consider that which is to come."

The Sphere spun away on the same flight path on which it had arrived

Paul floated into oblivion or a drunken coma. He had lost all sense of time, life, and pain as he drifted into a peaceful sleep.

He awoke suddenly with a start and a searing pain in his side. He was the child, Paul, again back in the room where he had been born.

"Mummy," the four-year-old was screaming from the top of the stairs, clutching at his right side in agony. Young Paul had awakened to something stabbing into his side, but now a dull throbbing pain drove him from his bed to the top of the stairs, where he tripped and fell over the pajama bottoms, around his ankles, and tumbled down the stairs, crashing headlong into the hall door.

He awoke on the rug in front of the fire, his father checking him over as his mother watched tearfully.

"I don't think he is badly injured. What happened, son?" his father tousled his hair.

"It's sore, Daddy, it's sore." Paul clutched at his right side.

"He's hurt his side in the fall," his father tried to console his wife.

"Ring the doctor, please, Dad," Paul's mum pleaded.

"I'm not awakening the neighbors at this hour of the night. If the pain is still there in the morning, I'll ring." Dad retorted.

"Please, Paul, please ring the doctor. I know wee Paul is in bad pain," Mum was in tears pleading.

Dad did not ring the doctor until 6 am from the next-door neighbor's house.

"It's appendicitis. Why the hell didn't you ring before now? Get back into John Jenkins and ring the ambulance. This lad's appendix is about to burst", Doctor Murray was seething.

All Paul could remember after that was being carried out on one of the dining room chairs, the blue light of the ambulance, the siren, and the priest by the trolley, as they wheeled him into the hospital, giving him the last rites of Extreme Unction.

The young lad awoke in the hospital cot in a daze, with all sorts of tubes and cables attached to him, but he heard through his pain. Mr. Savage, the Surgeon, spoke to his parents,

"Mr & Mrs. McGowan, your child died on the operating table with Peritonitis. But after 3 minutes, the staff miraculously revived him, and we had to give him a blood transfusion. You have a miracle child, dear people. He will need extra special care and attention, Mrs. McGowan, when he eventually leaves here."

Paul did not start school until he was seven years old, head and shoulders above his four-year-old classmates. His mother had not only given her son the care and attention the doctor prescribed, but she had 'mollycoddled' the boy she nearly lost and spoiled him with gifts on practically a weekly basis. It was as if she blamed herself for the lad's illness and his near death, and she tried her best to make up for it. Of course, not knowing any better, Paul took it all for granted.

"Spare the rod and spoil the child," his father preached at Paul's mother.

But Paul still awoke every weekend to a new toy or a bag of sweets lying at the end of his bed beside his black collie dog,

'Lucky,' who was the child's minder and bosom buddy. Paul loved both dearly but took his mother for granted, thinking all mums are like that.

Each morning, Lucky walked with Paul to the school gates where Paul would say his goodbyes, pat Lucky on the head, and send him home. When school ended, Lucky was waiting at the school gates, wagging his tail, and would walk home with Paul, but this time on the outside of the pavement to keep him off the road. When they saw Paul, his best mate Lucky was not far behind or in front of him.

Paul soon became the center of amusement, head and shoulders above his classmates, with his black sheepdog following him everywhere and him wearing red tropical shorts with bright green palm trees, which his aunt had sent him from America. The other kids squealed at him, 'Gooney Red Drawers,' a play on the word 'McGowan' linked to his attire. But Paul took no notice of the banter after school because Lucky was at the gate and dared any bully to come near him while Lucky was with him. His precious dog would have made a meal of their pants.

One day Paul found Lucky in the coal shed lying on his side, vomiting, "Daddy Lucky's sick."

"Luck has eaten poisoned meat, Son," his dad explained to a tearful Paul, "The sheep farmer in the back fields warned me he had put poison down, and I meant to tie the dog up. I'm so sorry, Lad."

Lucky died that day, as did Paul's joy of life and his whole world. He wouldn't experience that joy again until he was a young man of thirty-five.

"You're moving up three classes, McGowan. We need you ready for the qualifying exams. Tell your mother to come in and see me," the headmaster ordered a bewildered Paul, still grieving over his four-legged life-long friend the next day, "I'll sort this name-calling out as well; you're into long trousers next week, my Lad. Now you're playing with the Big Boys."

This move up, however, only exacerbated Paul's problem. The other boys were far more advanced than he was, and the nickname upgraded to "Dopey, Gooney Red Drawers."

So, it continued with no Lucky to protect him from being pushed around after school classes ended. He began to hate school and told his mum. She bought him a beautiful watch for his birthday and said he could wear it to school and then his classmates would envy him and try to be his friend. But the teacher confiscated it because Paul kept checking the time during the class and letting the other boys know how long it was to go before the break. After break time, the teacher discovered that the watch had been stolen out of the drawer when he came back.

Paul was slowly starting to realize the world he was living in now was not the world with his pal, Lucky, or the one he fantasized about in his 'Rupert the Bear,' annual that his mum had given him for Christmas.

This new world had poisoned his dog, stolen his watch, and now bullied him at school. "I don't like school, mum. Can I stay home with you?"

His mother, in exasperation, decided he needed to be home-schooled as well with grinds after his classes. She would also organize some Irish and Latin language lessons, which would gain the respect of his classmates and teachers.

The family gathered after the angelus at 6 pm for the Rosary praying in his mother's tongue.

Paul's mother spoke to the Parish Priest at her next Legion of Mary meeting and requested that her son become an Altar boy. As the Mass was in Latin, he would jolly well learn that,

'Ad Deum Qui Laetificat Juventutem Meam,' means 'To the God who gives joy to my youth" and learn what God was about in her youngster's life.

"There, that's settled. My son is going to be respected", she proclaimed to her husband at the tea table that evening.

One day the young lad's parents decided to visit a close friend of theirs, a missionary Priest on Sabbatical in Mount St. Clément's Retreat House, on the Cave hill Mountain. As the family walked through the grounds with the Priest towards the exit, he suddenly took off his biretta (priest's hat) and placed it on young Paul's head, saying,

"Don't be worrying about school, Son. God has plans for you. You will be a Priest someday."

The remark had more effect on the parents than on the young lad, suddenly blinded by the large hat covering his eyes. The prophetic word of the priest was the discussion of the parents all the way home.

Paul's mother was a native of Rossport in County Mayo, where everyone spoke Irish, and his father hailed from Ballymote in Sligo. So, the Irish language was used frequently at home, especially in fits of temper displayed by his mother. The native tongue was a way of admonishing her children, and it often became a precursor to a lash of the sally rod on the backs of the legs to scold the children. Paul did not entirely take to his mother's native tongue for that very reason. Still, he did manage to learn his prayers in Irish by continually repeating them or what he was later in life to know was 'Vain repetition.'

However, Latin was a very different matter. That was the language of the elite and the upper classes, and one could carry an air of importance with the ability to speak it.

Paul quickly began to gain the respect of his peers when he had learned all his prayers for confirmation and could pray in both Irish and in Latin. The parish Priest would often send over to the school for him to serve at ten o clock mass, as he was one of the best altar boys in the parish who knew all of the responses and how to function appropriately on the altar. Paul's only problem was that he hadn't a clue what he was praying.

A famous quote states that when God answers prayer, we depend on His ability; when He doesn't, He relies on ours.

Bobby Stevenson, a level 2 Senior College Student at St Malachy's College, was asked to give Paul his grinds. Bobby was fun. He taught Paul how to play draughts and chess, telling his mother to stimulate his brain. In between times, he had him working out puzzles, crosswords, and doing intelligence tests from qualifying papers that his teachers supplied to him. To Paul, it wasn't school. It was play and good fun. His educational prowess grew exponentially that year under the caring guidance of his new best friend, Bobby.

One thing that was picked up by all concerned was that Paul was a fast learner. He flew through his qualifying exam, finishing his paper 20 minutes before anyone else, much to the annoyance of the teacher overseeing the exam, who reported him to his headmaster. The headmaster was shocked when the results came out, and Paul's pass marks exceeded his classmates. The headmaster presented him with a prayer book, apologizing that there were no prayers in Irish or Latin in it.

He gained a scholarship to St Malachy's College, where his parents informed him that he would progress to Maynooth University and ordination to the Priesthood. Paul's only challenge with that plan was that it did not fit into his remit, but there were now seven years to work out a solution. So, he said nothing to the parents for the moment.

Off he went in September 1959, in his brand-new school uniform, Blazer and badge, skull cap, grey shirt and tie, trousers pressed like a tailor's dummy and shoe spit and polished, all bought from the tick man at 'Two Bob' a week. Paul was as proud as Punch and as terrified as Judy.

*****

The first time he ever heard the words 'Fenian' and 'Taig' was when he decided he could save himself a few pence and a half an hour's extra journey by alighting at an earlier stop long before the town center. He then would walk across Dover Street, which led him over the Shankill Road, one of the Protestant areas of Belfast, and then up towards the junction of the Crumlin and Antrim Roads at Carlisle Circus, followed by a short walk up to the College.

Those days were long before Northern Ireland would be torn apart by the Troubles and when the Falls Road, particularly the Upper Falls, had a 50% protestant population.

All the children played together, without the slightest bother of other religions. Harry West was the Unionist MP for West Belfast and was elected every term. No one commented that there wasn't a 'one man, one vote' policy. Mackie's Factory and Hughes Bakery on the Springfield Road did not employ Roman Catholics, nor did the Ormo Bakery on the Ormeau Road.

The McGowan Family never discussed those issues. The main problem discussed, and vehemently, was that his father and mother had to write to the bishop for permission to attend their best friend's wedding in the Church of Ireland at Broadway. The bishop did not grant the application. But, after much discussion at the dinner table, the parents decided that they would disobey the bishop and go anyway. They could always confess their 'Sin' to one of the priests at the Friday confessional and obtain absolution for their misdemeanor.

That did not work out as expected. Both parents were threatened in the confessional with possible expulsion from the church and given several novenas and litanies of the Rosary, which would be required to erase this severe breach of Church Protocol and grievous Hell Damming Mortal Sin.

Young Paul enquired what a Protestant was as the inflamed conversation unfolded to one of the neighbors at mealtime. Paul always played with the younger children and was concerned that he was sinning.

"Don't be daft, son," exclaimed his dad, "They just attend a different church building, and Catholics are not allowed in there."

"Why, what's in there?" asked Paul.

"Nothing, absolutely nothing, an altar, an organ, and some pews. No Statues, no Tabernacle, No Stations of the Cross, No Holy Water, no incense, but they do light candles on the altar," answered his dad.

"Sounds all right to me," quipped Paul, "You'd get through Mass pretty quick in that place."

His dad's answer satisfied Paul's curiosity but made him revisit the severe problem he had going to school that morning on the Shankill Road and change his mind about speaking to his parents about it.

He had been delighted with his new plan as he disembarked early from his bus and started the long walk-up Dover Street. The method allowed him an extra half hour in bed every morning, and he could save the bus fare and buy a Spider-Man Comic at the end of the week plus the Dandy and the Beano. *What a great shortcut. Why has no one else tried it?* he thought as he strolled along.

But the shortcut was suddenly cut short that morning when he heard behind him, "Fenian! Get the Taig Bastard! Come on, get that Effin Taig!"

"What? Who? Why? How did they know?" the questions spun in his head as Fright and Flight came to the rescue, and he took off like a greyhound out of the traps at Celtic Park.

55

Paul was a fast runner, and he was thankful his long, lean legs could outrun the pack of ravenous bigots on his tail. But a wrong turn and two streets later, he began to tire with severe pain in his right side.

The mob was catching him up, throwing bottles and stones after him. He had misjudged his directions in his panic and landed well above Carlisle Circus and the Antrim Road Junction.

The only solution was to try and enter the college by the teachers' entrance and car park on Crumlin Road. Thankfully the gate was still open, and he charged up the drive with the screaming mob hurling bottles, stones, and abuse at him from the gate.

He burst through the back door of the College exhausted, nearly flattening the Dean of Discipline, the infamous Fr. Purdy, as he made his way to the front gates of the College to dole out the daily lashings to the non-compliant, out of uniform, or late for school students. The back gate was out of bounds to all students under threat of expulsion as it was for vehicular traffic only and was a danger to those on foot. Also, Purdy could not staff it with his Rod of Discipline.

"What the Hell are you at McGowan" Purdy brought the rod down with a whack on the side of his black gown.

The little so-and-so remembers my name. I'm in trouble, Paul thought. *'From the Frying Pan into the Fire.'* "But- But-But"

"No buts, hand out. Six slaps for being out of bounds and grossly disheveled." **Whack**, the punishment of the Rod was exact and vigorous, "Now you already know that you are to enter via the Antrim Road Gate. Still, if I send you back through that howling mob, you shall arrive late if you can arrive at all by the time they finish. So, six more on the other hand for unpunctuality" - **Whack**.

"And you can have two hours of detention for crossing the Shankill Road and for bringing that mob of Orange thugs to the gates of this prestige college.

In those days, the luxury of child-line was not available. Punishment at school was a significant part of the curriculum, most especially doled out by the Priests, who seemed to delight in hammering the younger first-year students. If you did complain at home, you were more likely to be administered another thump for causing trouble at school.

However, the whole frightening episode and the conversation around the dinner table convinced Paul to relate the tragic affair to his parents. To his relief, his parents were very sympathetic, even to the effect that his father wished to visit this Bully of a Priest and give him a right going over.

"No, Dad, please don't. It will only become worse for me at college. I'm in enough trouble as it is".

"Are you sure, Son? I never thought these blasted clergy could be so cruel, and there must be something wrong in their heads. Tell you what, Son, you don't have to join that lot if you don't want to. How's that? You can be a Christian Brother instead".

Well, it was a bit better. One can leave the Brothers anytime you like, thought Paul.

Then his father explained to Paul that all 'Prods' were not the same, "Take Jim and his family, the wedding we attended,

57

they were distraught over the bishop's pedantic behavior." Paul's dad started again on his rant about the lousy clergy in the Catholic Church, 'Bla-Bla-Bla.'

And then suddenly - *inspiration* – he would take his son on his calls at the weekend around the Crumlin and Shankill Roads to meet some of his lovely 'Prod Clients.'

That Saturday, Paul came home with a new-found belief in the Protestant people of Belfast and a pocket filled with coins given to him by the sympathetic customers of his dad's after hearing of the young lad's frightening experience.

"You know what, Dad. I'd like to become one of those Protestants when I grow up. They have more money and nicer houses and cars than us".

"That's not altogether right, son," laughed his dad, "That's just what they call in Belfast, 'More Protestant looking.'"

*****

How has my Da become this wise so quickly?

Paul had considered his father as being a bit thick. Of course, all adults seemed thick to a boy of 11 years. One day, he had observed his father, an Insurance Agent, adding up columns of figures in Pound, Shillings, and Pence. His Dad seemed to run his pencil up the page and back down again, writing the totals at the bottom.

"Why are you doing that, Dad?" asked Paul.

"If you add it up, and then add it down, and achieve the same total, it is correct," explained his father.

Paul never had problems with his sums after that and moved his father up a notch in his edification process.

But his father's kind gestures, advice, and explanations, although accepted with enthusiasm, had not canceled Paul's planning for revenge and his bitterness towards this "Vlad the Impaler' at the college. He had already made up his mind that vengeance would be his, and he'd eventually sort Purdy at some time soon.

DISCOVERING BELFAST

The winter of the heavy snowfalls and snowball fights had broken out on St Malachy's playing fields – all good innocent fun. But Purdy and his band of Senior Prefects had decided to end the ungentlemanly behavior of the first-year students.

During Purdy and his cronies' invasion of the playing fields, Paul and his pals were throwing snowballs from the perimeter of the trees and were able to slip away unnoticed. Purdy and his lackeys commenced herding the offending Junior students into a line for a proper thrashing

At a safe distance down the lane, Paul looked back. The punishment of the first-year students had commenced as they extended trembling hands already numb with the cold for the unmerciful lash of the cane.

"Listen, Lads, do you think we could whack him on the back of the head from here?" panted Paul.

"Naw, too far," replied Joe (Paul's closest college companion), as he threw a snowball he had just made, and it fell quite a long way short.

One of the sports that Paul excelled at was Handball. He had played it on the streets of Belfast with his friends since he was a nipper. On his first day at college, he had joined the handball Alley fraternity, which recognized him as having enormous potential. His stepbrother, Gerard, had won many medals at the same college as a Handball champion. So, it was a family thing.

"I think I can reach him with a bit of help," smiled Paul as he pushed a large stone into the giant snowball that he had just made.

He launched it into the air with a vengeful heart and all the brute force that he could muster. The missile uncannily hit the target, the back of the Dean's head, who fell to the ground with a yell to the delight of the 1st year onlookers.

Not only was the air blue, but the language emanating from this 'Man of the Cloth' was also X-rated and neither in Irish nor Latin, "Get that Effin little Bastard what threw that, and I'll cut his Effin B*lls off..!"

The students were still rocking with laughter.

"You are 'Damn well' dismissed," screamed Purdy at the first-year assembly, as he placed a white handkerchief over the wound on his head and was helped away, limping, by his band of Prefects.

Paul and his mates had meanwhile fled like Jack Flash, but it did not take long to ascertain who the culprit had been.

Paul was the hero of the school for a whole week. He enjoyed his month's suspension from the school immensely, deciding not to say a word to his parents and watch for the postman until he could retrieve the letter from the college principal outlining the details of an unprovoked attack by their son on a senior member of staff. He read the letter with glee by the banks of the River Lagan as he ate the lunch his loving mother had prepared for him before she went to her work.

"This is great," he declared as he walked along the Lagan towpath.

I wonder whether anyone would notice if I were to extend the term of suspension.

Eight months later, Paul was caught and hauled before the College Principal, Fr. Walter Larkin, who would eventually become Parish Priest of St Paul's during the Troubles.

That month, a campaign was in place to find vocations for the Priesthood in the college. So, Paul had hatched a plan for his defense. He explained to the annoyed Principal that he had repented his actions during the first month of imposed suspension. In the beautiful surroundings of the Lagan Valley, Paul had acquired a deep desire for prayer, fasting, and meditation. He explained to the wide-eyed Priest that he decided to extend his period of reflection to practice and prepare himself for the tasks that Ordination into the Priesthood would carry. The principal swallowed it hook, line, and sinker. He was in awe of such faith in one of his students and gave Paul access to the Senior's library to study.

Paul decided that if he could fool a senior man of the cloth so quickly, he did not see the point of joining such a bunch of misfits and would seek his future career in a more fruitful venture.

During his self-imposed absence from the college, he had put his time to good use, learning his way around Belfast City. There were very few streets that he did not know by now.

At the start of his leave of absence, he had informed his mother that, because of the upsurge in attacks upon the students, it was no longer compulsory to wear the school uniform for anyone who felt threatened.

He now left the house in Jeans, jumper, and coat in the morning, hiding his schoolbag in the coal shed at the back of the house on his way out, and just bringing his lunch box. His real education began at the University of Life on the streets of Belfast. Schoolwork did not fit into Paul's schedule for the foreseeable future, as he planned to see and learn more about Belfast City.

His father died of a stroke following an extended illness when Paul was fourteen. His mother had already gone back to her job as a waitress to feed the family, consisting of Paul and his two younger sisters. The young lad and his siblings had learned to cycle proficiently in Mayo on their aunts' bikes when on holidays. So, he persuaded his mother that if she bought him a bicycle, she would save on bus fares, and he could help out by getting a job as a message boy after school and on Saturdays.

His Mum bought the bicycle for her son. As he had committed the street map of Belfast to memory during his 'Mitching Off' period, there was not a street or road that he could not place. All of this street knowledge was put to good use when Brian McCann, the Pharmacist at the bottom of the Whiterock Road, gave him his first job as a message boy.

"Your son completes his workload much faster than the previous fellow,'" declared Brian, the pharmacist, to Paul's mother. He increased the ten bob a week to twelve and six, an extra half a crown because he didn't have to give Paul bus fares to deliver prescriptions or collect orders from the wholesalers.

Paul learned his first lesson in Entrepreneurial Enterprise in McCann's Chemist shop. He had overheard a customer ask Brian for a packet of condoms. The devout catholic chemist was aghast at such a request. He told the customer that he would be better asking a Protestant Chemist on the Shankill Road and that no self-respecting Catholic Chemist offered such disgusting wares. The customer's reply left the poor chemist in shock, "It's OK, Brian, I'll get them from Mick the Barber tomorrow. It's just that he is closed on a Monday".

"What are condoms?" asked Paul innocently. "You're too young for questions like that," was the stern reply.

No, I'm not, thought Paul; *maybe it's time I got my hair cut.*

Mick the Barber was very accommodating. He tried to explain what 'Something for the weekend' meant simply to the confused young lad.

"Condoms are banned by the Catholic Church under pain of Mortal Sin, so the chemists on the Falls will not supply them. I buy mine from a friend on the Shankill and make plenty of sales. But your man takes a big cut out of my profit," declared Mick, "I wish I knew the chemist wholesaler who supplies them? My brother plays in a showband and could smuggle thousands of them over the border into the South and sell them at the dances".

"Well, I go to all the wholesalers for Brian," grinned Paul broadly.

"Great! Good Lad. Find out who sells them and let me know," Mick's grin was even broader.

"No Problem." Paul had made friends with the other message boys and would enquire.

"Can you supply Barbershops?" Paul enquired meekly at the appropriate wholesaler.

"No, Son, you need to go to Sawyers for hair products. You should know that already." The man at the wholesalers wiped the counter with a damp cloth.

"No, no, it's a Barber friend of mine on the Falls, and he wants condoms," Paul's retort was a little louder than he intended. The small group of message boys began tittering in the corner.

"Come into the office and talk it over with the Sales Manager," the compliant counter hand lifted the flap after he had spoken to someone on the intercom, much to the chagrin of the tittering group in the corner.

"Who is this Barber on the Falls?" a ruddy round face smiled up at him from a mahogany desk, "Are we about to break the condom embargo on the Falls Taig Road?" he roared with laughter along with the counter assistant.

He looked Paul over for a moment weighing him up, and then looked back at his cluttered desk, "Yeah, no problem, young man. We would be delighted to supply your barber friend. Please bring in the order on his billhead and tell him to give us a ring to set up his account. One month's credit and discount for bulk purchases, that sound OK?"

Paul related to an ecstatic Mick later that afternoon, the conversation which had taken place at the wholesaler. Mick offered him five shillings a week and free haircuts if he would collect the orders, as he would not dare venture into that part of town and was too busy anyway.

Paul was delighted with his newly- found negotiating skills; *I wonder if I could sell them too? What are they for, I wonder?*

The University of Life was teaching Paul more of the practicalities of life than his schooling. He voiced this opinion to his mother one evening after passing his junior certificate to the amazement of his teachers. She suggested that he needed and would probably do better in a mixed and non-denominational College.

"What's that?" quizzed her son.

"Boys & girls, and different cultures and religions will give you a better outlook on life. St Malachy's is very introverted, and you don't want to be a Priest anymore," his mother explained, thinking she would expand his horizons somewhat.

Shaftesbury Tutorial College was a complete culture shock for Paul, and it looked more like the students ran it than the teachers. He asked one of the older girls for a Christmas dance after his friend advised him to pick an ugly one who would accept his invitation.

The haughty reply didn't upset Paul, "No thanks, and I wouldn't dance with a child."

"Sorry Missus," replied Paul, "I hadn't noticed your condition," a reply that introduced him to the fist of the girl's boyfriend.

As Paul picked himself up from the floor, he thought that possibly his mother had made a mistake, this time, about Shaftesbury Tutorial College widening his outlook. The only thing that widened was his sore jaw.

"Ok, Ok," his mother was becoming exasperated, "You have only passed English Literature and French in your GCE. So, you are not progressing at college. "You may start work. There is a commis-chef position in the Glen Machan Tower hotel. I know the owner, and I'll see if he will take you on. He owes me a favor anyway."

Paul got the job without an interview and turned up the next week to start washing lettuce, peeling spuds, and learning his trade from the ground up at five pounds ten shillings a week. He lost the first ten shillings the day he started when Teddy Foster, another commis-chef, told him he could fry ice cream.

"Aye right!" exclaimed Paul, "I'm from West Belfast, but I'm not that thick."

"I'm from East Belfast, and I bet yaw ten shillings out of your first wage packet," Teddy drawled.

"Go on then," Paul replied.

That day he learned his first lesson from the resourceful Teddy, who dipped a scoop of ice cream into the batter, rolled it in breadcrumbs, and chucked it in the deep fat fryer.

"That's ten-bob you owe me this Friday," laughed Teddy, as he pulled the hot 'Helado Frito' out of the fryer, "That's your first lesson. You don't know squat, so keep your mouth shut."

He and Teddy became bosom pals, and Paul kept his mouth shut and learned to be a chef.

One day he was in the kitchen on his own, and the head chef was sleeping off an early morning boozing session in the changing room.

The Boss walked in, "Where's Willie?"

"I don't know, Boss. I think he went out for a smoke."

"He did my backside. I heard he played cards in his room with his drunken pals all night. Where is he?" "Willie! Where, the heck, are you, man? We have a busload of tourists just arrived."

The boss ran into the changing room to find Willie out cold on top of the laundry.

"Paul the a-la-carte is off. It's a 'Table D'ote' menu tonight, steak, chicken curry, tuna salad or cod & chips, OK, you're in charge", the boss rushed up to tell the Restaurant Manager.

Shortly after, Tommy, the head waiter, approached the bain-marie counter, pinned his order on the board, and called out, "Chef, Twelve sirloins, six medium-rare, three well done, & 3 blue."

"I only have 10, Tommy," explained Paul.

"I said 12, Chef, bone two off that side of beef that came in this morning."

"It's too fresh, Tommy, and it needs to hang for a while."

"Bone the blasted thing, man. If Willie were here, he'd sort it." Tommy hurried from the kitchen.

Paul sent the steaks out, and the head waiter immediately returned with two fresh ones, "They're too tough."

Paul flung a pot at Tommy, who ducked laughing.

"I'll sort the Orange Pricks out, coming in here in their regalia, bloody marching bands. I hate Northern Ireland".

"What on earth is the matter with you, Tommy?" Paul was surprised at the remark.

Tommy stared over at Paul, "I was born in England. My Dad's a Northern Prod, and Ma's an Irish Catholic, and I don't know what I am. Every year, there is fighting in our house at the marching season, and I want a quiet life when I go home".

Tommy still lived with his parents at the age of twenty-two. He put up with his parental relatives from both the Orange and the Green sides of the divide. Poor Tommy had taken his mother's part and had fallen foul of his protestant cousins.

"Tommy tell the punters, I have a nice curry or Tuna Salad, and we'll give them a free glass of wine," Paul felt sorry for Tommy's predicament.

"Be the Book. I know what I'll give them." Tommy fired the steaks on the ground and stamped them with his polished Beatle Boot. He then threw the steaks back under the grill for a few minutes, placed them neatly on a silver platter with some piped potato, cucumber, tomato, and garnish, and danced out of the kitchen. He came back an hour later with a five-pound note, "A drink for the Chef from the 'Orange Men.' The steaks were perfect."

Time for me to move on, thought Paul; *I don't need to live with this rubbish. There has to be a better way to earn money.*

When he was twelve, he had read his first book on 'Positive Thinking, 'Bring out the Magic in your mind,' by Al Koran, a television conjurer. Using the methods and advice on taking positive action in one's belief patterns taught in that book, he started to look for ideas and ways to improve his life. After meeting a guy in the hotel bar who was making more than a week's wages selling soft drinks at the weekend, he borrowed £40 from his mother and bought a van.

A friend told him there was a company in Newry looking for agents. Paul, by now, was not afraid to negotiate. At the age of nineteen, he walked into the office of Tom Garland, the MD of the Newry Mineral Water company, and asked for a week's credit.

"I need a bank reference," declared Tom.

"I don't have a bank." answered the cheeky intruder.

"What age are you, kid?" *There is something about this kid,* thought Tom.

"19, Sir."

Seems to have the proper manner too? Tom weighed Paul up for a moment, "Is that your van out there? How much have you paid for it?"

"£40, Sir."

"Bring in the logbook and your driver's license," Tom wrote down Paul's particulars off the license and threw the logbook in his desk drawer. He pressed the intercom, "Gerry, give this lad forty quid's worth of mixed soft drinks." He turned to Paul, "You've big Cahoonas, Kid, walking in here with a smile. You are back here with the money and any empty bottles in a week. We are members of the bottle exchange and can accept all company empties. If you're not back, I'm selling that van of yours. Best of luck, kid."

Tom was still shaking his head as Paul left; *Big Cahoonas! That kid will go far.*

Paul was back in Newry the next day with a van load of empty bottles and the cash he owed.

"What on earth! How did you get rid of that lot in half a day?" Tom was in shock.

"Easy," replied Paul, "I went into Turf Lodge estate. Six kids were playing football on the first street, so I asked them if they wanted a shilling each and free pop, but they could only drink it on the van. There is only so much fizzy pop a kid can drink. I just told them to knock every door on each side of the street and say 'Lemonade,' "And whatever the lady says, like, 'Is that Briggs?' or 'Maine?' or 'Braid?' or 'Thompsons?' just answer 'Yes,' take their empties, collect the money and bring back their order. I sold the lot in an hour and a half, sir."

"Gerry, come in here," Tom spoke into the intercom, "This kid's going to teach us a thing or two about marketing. Told you, didn't I, 'Big Cahoonas'"

"Tell you what, kid, leave your van here. I will lend you a bigger van and give you a week's credit. Open that bank account. You're in business."

Paul had his bank account opened within a few weeks, traded in his little Bedford van for a better, bigger model on HP, returned the loaned van to Newry, and no one would ever order him around anymore.

He had heard from a friend that a school meals transport company was looking for owner-drivers. He applied and was given a run in North Belfast, Monday to Friday, and that fitted in well with his soft drinks business on Thurs and Friday nights and all-day Saturday.

While on the school meals run, he suffered a puncture outside of Rubber & Plastic products in North Belfast. George Allen came out with a wheel spider to help him take the wheel off, as the nuts were too tight.

"You're delivering around Belfast, are you?" asked George, and with Paul's acquiescent nod, he suggested, "Call in when you have finished your run, and I'll give you some deliveries for West Belfast and the Dock area."

George then introduced Paul to his partner, Tom Simms, "Drop over to Dunlop Angus," said Tom, "They deliver to the same people we do, and you may as well deliver their supplies also. They're looking for a good man. Here's my card, tell them I sent you. I used to work for that particular company."

What's going on?" thought Paul, "I must have an angel or someone looking after me.

This fortunate encounter with these two men would be instrumental in helping him establish one of the first privately owned logistics transport companies specializing in home deliveries in both Britain and Ireland.

*****

"George Millar up the West Circular has the Avon Cosmetics delivery contract, and he needs someone for west Belfast," A friend at Rubber & Plastic Products one day announced to Paul.

He immediately called on George, who was relieved to find someone prepared to deliver into that part of the city, where there was potential rioting.

Eventually, when George decided to end his contract, Paul rang Avon. The traffic manager agreed to meet Paul and visit his depot the following week. Paul did not mention that he had no depot and only had one van.

He phoned his friend, Ron, who had given him the school meals run, "Hi Ron. I need to borrow your depot and your ten vans for a little while early Monday morning. How much will it cost me?"

"What are you up to, Paul?" Ron was curious.

"I believe I can swing the Avon Cosmetics contract with a bit of bluff. The traffic manager is calling over to see Northern Ireland Carriers and a couple of other groupage companies, as George Millar is packing it in."

"You can swing it? How will you do that, Kid, with one van?"

"No eleven, your ten plus your depot in Stranmillis. I'll share the deliveries with you, as I can't do them all." Paul's enthusiasm always impressed Ron.

Go for it, Kid," laughed Ron, "I'll be working for you on Monday. See you at the office, Boss."

Paul picked up Avon's traffic manager, 'David Fagg' (*real name*), at the airport in his newly polished Jaguar and took him to 'His Depot.'

Ron came out of the office to greet the pair, "Mr. McGowan, I delayed the vans from going off early this morning as I thought Avon's traffic manager would like to look them over first."

"You realize, Mr. Fagg, that we are an integral part of your business already as we are the only people that George Millar has to venture into the more dangerous areas of Belfast. We employ drivers from those areas who are known to the locals." Paul exuded confidence as he showed off the fleet of Ron's vans.

"It's David, Paul. I think we will be on first-name terms from now on. Thank you for your kind hospitality. You have the job. Please, take me back to the airport. I was very nervous coming to Northern Ireland & their 'Troubles.' " David Fagg was not looking forward to going to N.I. Carriers on the Grosvenor Road, or anywhere else in the country for that matter except the airport.

While Paul negotiated his first significant contract, he watched Ron grinning from ear to ear.

*****

Many years later, Paul's young son was playing with Lego. Paul now had an established limited company and signed a contract to deliver Encyclopaedia Britannica throughout Ireland. He needed light goods to fill out his vans. There was a UK telephone number on the Lego carton. Paul rang the number,

"Hello, is that the Lego Factory?"

The polite female answered. "Yes. The distribution comes from here. How can I be of help?"

Paul had honed his technique and was brazen,

"I am ringing about your appalling service to Ireland."

"WHAT!" the lady seemed rather upset.

"I shall put you through to that department and kindly hold the line."

John Harvey-Jones here. How can I be of assistance?" an even politer polished voice. Paul felt a bit ashamed of his controversial approach but carried on, "Mr. Harvey Jones, I was at the Toy Fair in the Park Avenue Hotel, and your customers were complaining about your delivery service to Ireland," Paul lied through his teeth.

"Who exactly are you, might I ask?" came the response.

"The person who can solve your problem. I have a van in every town in Ireland once a week, and would that help?" Paul had him hooked.

"Well, unfortunately, our present carrier is sometimes a bit slower than expected. Give me some reference contacts of yours to speak with."

Paul gave him several UK companies, "Avon Cosmetics. Amway Corporation, Betterware, Pippadee, Ideal Toys, Triang Pedigree, and we deliver for most mail-order companies. Does that help?"

"Thank you. I will revert to you within the week," was the curt reply.

Half an hour later, the phone rang, "John Harvey-Jones here. Meet me at my office in Wrexham in the morning, Mr. McGowan."

Paul rang his agent Peter Gill in York, "Peter, pick me up in Leeds Bradford Airport in the morning. We are going to Wrexham."

"To see whom? Peter replied.

"Some bloke from the Lego Place, John Harvey-Jones."

"WHO?" gasped Peter, "That's the chairman of ICI, and their factory is in Wrexham. You blooming' Irish, how do you do it?"

Paul and Peter closed the deal the next day. And in like manner, Paul kept building his company up and up like the Tower of Babble until it toppled.

The 'Big Cahoonas' did not do much when he lost everything, including his beautiful bungalow in Ballyclare.

*****

The Sphere was spinning again above Paul's head. "The Almighty blessed you with the gift of communication, Dear One. You have both used and abused that gift, never once giving thanks to the One who was blessing you."

"This cannot be real. Wake up, Paul, blast you!" but Paul did not wake up.

"Watch, remember and evaluate both the positive and the hostile forces at work in your life, as your appetite and thirst were unable to be satisfied in the emptiness of the world," The spinning globe continued to admonish Paul, "You tried the broken cisterns, but ah, the waters failed. Even as you stooped to drink, they fled and mocked you as you wailed. A human heart will thirst in taking, but that thirst is quenched only in giving. Watch and learn from the past."

Paul drifted off back into his past life, viewing the things that he wished to leave buried and in no way to bring them back to his remembrance. He watched, embarrassed, shocked, sorry, and ashamed.

*****

"Blessed is the man that walked not in the counsel of the ungodly," Psalm1:1 (NKJ)

Before the angel left him following his review, he communicated once more by sending Paul back again into time. He further explained that time only exists on earth, not in Eternity which is forever present. God could enter the past to heal memories and into the future to prevent tragedy.

"Paul, you have a purpose in the Kingdom Work. Those before you have run the race, falling as you have, so many times on their journey but arising with renewed strength. You will replenish your power as the eagle because of the wind beneath your wings. Catch that wind of the Spirit, and you will ride all storms. Your review ends with one more session, where you failed to catch that wind even though you were rescued and set again upon the mountaintop. Watch, remember, learn to follow the correct voice of the many in your head.

Paul was once again spinning back in time. He was age 27.

He owned depots in Dublin, Ballyclare Antrim, and East Kilbride, Scotland.

He had agents in Manchester, York, Birmingham, and the Isle of Dogs in London and happened to be in London for the first time in his life.

Big Colin from his agent's Depot had some business to finish in London and offered to show Paul around later. He seemed to know everyone whom he met.

"No, Paul, don't go near the west end. You don't need a show, and you need the sights. We are going to the East End. I'll keep you right, my Paddy Friend," said Big Colin as they entered the Black Cat Strip Club in SoHo.

Colin went to the front to see the show. Paul, who immediately was revolted by the place, went to the bar for a drink.

"Your beer is rubbish," complained Paul to the barman.

"Take it or leave it, Paddy. You're in a wine bar", the barkeep snarled at him.

"Shush!" The guy behind Paul had his finger to his lips, "Bottle of Merlot, Alex old chap, and two glasses. It's my friend's first visit here, and I'm sure you don't want to lose new punters. Follow me, young Irish Friend," he winked at Paul. The accent was like Lord Haw-Haw.

"Stuck up, English Prude," thought Paul as he followed him to a table.

"I'm Seamus from south Armagh," the accent had changed dramatically.

"How'd you do that?" gasped Paul.

"I've gone 'AWAL,' and the army wants to ship me off to Belfast, where I'll get shot. My mate is taking me to Germany tomorrow in his truck. The Irish are not allowed to serve in Northern Ireland, but I joined up using my aunt's address in London, and they think I'm English."

The tongues loosened, and the Irish banter began as the night wore on.

Suddenly three black faces peered down at them,

"Eff off back to your Irish Bog, Paddy."

Seamus found his English accent very quickly,

"I'll eff off to my place, old chap if you eff off back to the jungle where you came from."

At that, the huge seven-foot giant grabbed a jug of water off the table and lunged it straight at Seamus, who ducked like an acrobat, and the pitcher split open the head of the customer at the following table, covering both Paul and Seamus in blood. Next thing Big Colin, a hulk of a Rugby Player, smashed a chair over the giant's head, smacked his two mates in the nether regions, grabbed Paul, and headed for the stairs to be met by the bouncers who held them until the Police arrived within minutes.

They grabbed Paul and threw him into the police van on the accusation of the guy who threw the jug. They brought Paul to the Police Station, telling Colin to make himself scarce. Paul was charged with GBH and thrown in a cell. At 3 am, a shabbily dressed vagrant entered the cell with two uniforms behind,

"Paul Adrian McGowan, Falls Road Belfast?" the stranger spoke in a polished Brit accent.

"No, Ballyclare." *Who was this weird person?* The voice did not fit with the appearance.

"I repeat 'Are you the Paul Adrian McGowan from the Falls Road."

"Yes! What the hell do you want with me?"

"Take him, lads." The uniforms grabbed Paul and dragged him to a table in a cell further up. The vagrant sat down and put his folder on the table.

"Tell me about these murders in which you are involved. If you come clean and give us the names of your accomplices, this all goes away, and you move to protective custody."

"I've had enough of this bullshit," Paul rose to his feet, only to be pushed violently back down by the two Uniforms behind him, "Phone my cousin, "Chief Superintendent Brian Lally in RUC Headquarters Strand Road Londonderry. He'll give you my CV and my standing in the community and that I run a successful haulage business."

The vagrant's face suddenly broadened to a smile. "That's OK, lads. You can leave now. Bring Paul and me a cup of tea and don't spit in it; he's no Fenian," he addressed the two men behind Paul.

"Oh, so you know Brian Lally," Paul felt suddenly relieved.

"No, never heard of him." The vagrant smiled across the table at Paul.

"What in blazes are you playing at?" Paul was by now very agitated.

"Settle down, Lad. I'm just doing my job. I'm an undercover MI6 officer, and I heard that they picked this Mick up in the Black Cat for GBH, so here I am."

He went to the door, "George, bring Paul's file in now, thanks."

After he read the file, "Are they the witnesses?" he roared with laughter, "Two druggies and an Arms dealer?"

"What do you mean?" said Paul.

"Our boys were watching them tonight. That's who told me about you. These three will be in clink long before your case comes up. We have them under surveillance to find their top man. Where is your cousin stationed, by the way?"

"Londonderry. I already told you."

"That's not the word the 'RA' would have called it. Now, why does a man from the Falls Road refer to Derry as Londonderry?"

"Because that's what it's called." Paul had thought that the English would not know of 'Derry,' so was prompted to call it 'Londonderry.'

"Not by the 'RA' it's not. Tell you what, mate. The Met has stitched you up. Sue their asses off when you are acquitted."

"Can you not tell them about your guys who saw the incident?" asked Paul.

"Oh no, we can't break cover, not even to the Met." Don't be worried you'll beat this and get yourself a few quid into the bargain." The MI 6 officer shook Paul's hand and left. Paul never drank the tea.

As he was pushed back into his cell, he broke into tears and fell against the metal table, which was bolted to the floor, knocking a book onto the bunk. It fell open. Paul picked up the book and read,

The Lord is my shepherd; I shall not want. He makes me lie down in green pastures: He leads me by the still waters.

His eyes fell upon verse 4 of the Gideon Bible in his shaking hands,

Though I walk through the valley of the shadow of death, I will fear no evil; for thou art with me; thy rod and staff they comfort me.

Paul cried himself to sleep with the Bible on his chest.

*****

The following day he appeared in the dock in court.

"Have you any representation, Sir?" the judge looked with disdain over the top of his half-rimmed spectacles at Paul.

The police removed his shoelaces, belt, and tie, and Paul was trying to hold up his trousers, unshaven and with his shirt covered in dry blood.

"The solicitor the police sent to my cell wanted me to sign a confession, and when I wouldn't, he walked away" Paul felt his voice trembling.

"Read the charges, bailiff. How do you plead?"

"Not guilty, your honor." Paul was shaking visibly now.

"You are a flight risk, and so I cannot set bail. I remand you in custody until your trial date. Take the prisoner down."

Paul's legs could hardly support his body, and he thought he was fainting from exhaustion. Just at that, a door opened to the right of the Bench, and a Dapper little man with Jewish headgear walked in, followed by Big Colin,

"I am representing Mr. McGowan, your Honour."

He had a cheque in his hand, "I believe we can set bail at say £10,000.

The Judge looked at the cheque.

"That will do fine, David. How are you today?"

"Fine, see you later at the club." The dapper chap replied, beckoning Paul.

"The defendant is free to go. See you at the club, David."

Paul collected his clothing from the police and followed Colin and David into the back of a waiting Rolls Royce parked outside the courthouse.

"I'm not finished with those bastards yet," said David as he got into the rear of the Rolls with Big Colin and Paul, "Off you go, Victor. Let's get this young man cleaned up."

"David's father came to Israel on the Exodus Ship in 1948, and the British Army interned the family in a concentration camp. His father died in David's arms, and there is no love lost between him and the British Establishment. He and his mother were released and moved to London. He is one of the top Barristers in the City and a very close friend of mine, Paul," explained Colin.

"Which is more than I can say for you, Colin, bringing this lad to the Black Cat indeed. That's some friend! What's your wife going to say about this."

"I won't tell if you don't."

A year later, Paul received £400 damages against the Met for false arrest plus all of his expenses and a week's stay in a top London Hotel, which David insisted he booked into at David's cost as the MET would pay his claim for all expenses. The court suspended the two arresting Met officers from duty, and the court also apologized to Paul through his solicitor for the inexcusable treatment of a British Citizen.

The Angel was communicating again,

"*Understand the message in the book which you knocked off the table in your cell?*".

Paul looked down again. He was back in the cell staring at the open Gideons Bible in his still shaking hands,

The Lord is my Shepherd; I shall not want. Paul read the complete psalm 23 in tears of sorrow and understanding.

"Be warned, my child, the wrong voices can close your mind to the things of God."

*****

Paul found himself in a van at the top of the Shankill Road as he felt the fear in his stomach. It was August 1983. Paul's company had gone bankrupt, and he was driving a van. The depot manager asked him to do the West Belfast Avon run as the driver had called in sick. After leaving the depot, Paul suddenly realized that the Shankill Road was on the list.

"Hi, Paul, Paul! How are you, buddy? Big Roy, an ex-employee of Paul's, ran across from the Woodvale Park carrying a guitar. What are you doing here? I'll give you a hand down the Shankill, and everyone knows me. You'll be safe enough with me."

Paul's heart sank. Roy was either a member of the UDA or UVF paramilitaries.

"What have you been up to, Roy?" asked Paul.

"Since you sacked me, do you mean?" Roy laughed.

"Sorry about that, but you deserved it, Roy," Paul felt uneasy.

"I know, mate. No hard feelings. I went to Bible College, and I am a youth Pastor. I'm working with a bunch of Catholic and Protestant kids. That's them with my helpers over in the Park. They are great Kids and get on well together. Tell me this, Paul? Was Jesus a Catholic or a Protestant?"

"I think He was a Jew, Roy."

"He was also the Son of God who became the Son of Man. He was neither a Prod nor a Taig, so why are we fighting?"

"I'm not fighting, Roy."

"No, I don't mean 'You,' I mean the Taigs and the Prods."

"I don't know, Roy. I wish we could find a way to end it."

"We can. I will call up for you on Sunday. Do you still live in that nice bungalow in Ballyclare?"

"No, Roy, I lost it. Here's my address." Paul handed Roy a used envelope with his address on it." "What's on this Sunday?"

"You'll see. An answer to your question." "Don't worry, the Lord has a nicer house for you, and he just has not told you about it yet."

Roy collected Paul that Sunday and took him to the Assemblies of God, Bethshan Tabernacle, and pastor Bob Edgar was preaching.

"Welcome, Everyone, especially if you are here for the first time. Bethshan means 'The House of Peace,' which the country seeks earnestly.

Whether you are a Roman Catholic or a roaming Protestant, we don't mind here, but please understand that you are roaming the wrong roads if Jesus is not your companion. You are going to meet him here tonight".

Paul's life changed that night. A huge weight lifted off his shoulders as he cried his way to the cross in Pastor Edgar's Office. The Pastor gave him a book, "The Happiest People on Earth" by Demos Shakarian,

"My brother-in-law, Hector Crory, gave me that book during the week. He told me that a young Catholic man would come to the Lord in this place tonight. God's hand is on that young man. Give him that book. That book, Paul, is from the Lord to you."

Paul took the book home and read it many times. He gave it to his best friend, John Lyons, in Donaghadee, who read it and placed it on his bookshelf. John's son, a Believer, was killed in a motorbike accident in England the following week.

People wondered why they were not sorrowful at the funeral. His parents knew that he was in Glory and would see him again someday.

However, a day later, John phoned Paul in uncontrollable tears, "Paul, I'm sorry I forgot about that book of yours and put it on my bookshelf."

"That's alright, John. You are supposed to pass it on until it reaches the right person, and you are that person."

"But - that is the point, Paul. I received a parcel from my son this morning, and he posted it the day that he died. In it was a copy of your book, 'The Happiest People on Earth,' and a note, 'Dad, please find these people and help them.'

Next week, I'm going to the Stormont Hotel to one of their Breakfasts. Will you come with me? ---- The Stormont with me, ----- the Stormont with me...." John's voice faded away as Paul spun back to the present.

"Make sure you are listening to the right voice." The Angel disappeared, and Paul awoke.

It was dawn. The sun was rising, and the evil yellow waters turned crimson red in the morning sunlight. He heard the song of a thrush high in a tree praising God.

The world was beautiful again. The pain in his head had vanished. He placed his hand on the back of his head, expecting to find matted blood and a bleeding gash. His head was clear – no gash and no blood. He rose to his knees and prayed in the morning light to the song of the thrush.

He was stone-cold sober and thanked God that he was alive with a newfound peace within his heart, that peace that transcends all understanding. God opened a new chapter in his life, and the joy of the Lord had found a place in Paul's heart once more.

He eventually made his way back to Dublin, where he had found work, and began to try to put his life back together. However, it would take him many challenging years, traveling many wrong roads, until he realized that he could not walk any of them without Jesus.

Years later, the truth emerged about Peter. A close friend rang Paul from the North and related that he was vindicated. Shirley had divorced Peter, who was now in jail for child abuse. He became a clergyman ordained in Bobby Millar's denomination in the USA.

Bobby Millar had died suddenly.

Sam had succumbed to a tumor on the brain and was seriously ill.

Ron had suffered several heart attacks and a stroke.

Norm and his wife had gone to Spain and died in a car accident.

Pastor Denis had contracted some strange illness (the person who rang Paul did not elaborate).

But, said the caller, Paul McGowan probably had a story to share and should write a book.

Several years later, in 2016, Paul suffered three strokes.

After five days of tests, the doctor who admitted him came up to the Ward, "Gentlemen," she clapped her hands, and the eight patients, including Paul, sat up in their beds,

"Word has reached me that you have all been asking about Paul in the bed here. Is he a Priest or a Minister? Is he going to die? Because everyone who visits him prays for him. Well, I have your answer, and with Paul's permission, I will give it to you.

He was in a serious condition when he arrived here five days ago after suffering several strokes during the night. His Right Carotid Artery was 80% blocked, and the left was 68% blocked. We did not believe that he would survive and expected that, at best, we would not see any improvement for at least six weeks.

We sent him down for an MRI scan this morning. The left artery is completely clear, and the right is 20%. We are releasing him today, after only five days. Now, Gents, it wasn't the aspirin, the medication, medical staff, or the medical attention that healed him, and it was the prayers at his bedside.

Thank you, Paul, for giving us all hope in Wexford Hospital. You should write your story in a book to give others hope."

I wonder should I write that book? Thought Paul as he left the hospital.

Perhaps God wants others to know that He is not a 'Religion,' nor an 'Uncaring Entity' out there somewhere in this vast universe, He is our 'Abba,' our Dad, who loves us, but we need the proper connection to come to Him – FAITH in Jesus, His Son.

As Paul left the hospital, the Angel seemed to speak once more into Paul's soul for the last time,

"Vision without Action is a Daydream.

Action without Vision is a Nightmare.

Listen to the right voice, Paul."

Paul was later to become one of the 'Happiest People on Earth,' and he did write that book. But that is another story for another time.

<u>The Beginning.</u>